# Rav Chesed
## The Life and Times of
## Rabbi Haskel Lookstein

*Rafael Medoff*

# Rav Chesed
## The Life and Times of Rabbi Haskel Lookstein

*Rafael Medoff*

KTAV Publishing House, Inc.

Library of Congress Cataloging-in-Publication Data

Medoff, Rafael, 1959-
    Rav chesed : the life and times of Rabbi Haskel Lookstein / by Rafael
Medoff.
        p. cm.
    Includes bibliographical references.
    ISBN 978-1-60280-043-4
    1. Lookstein, Haskel. 2. Rabbis—New York (State)—New York—
Biography.
3. Ramaz School (New York, N.Y.) 4. Congregation Kehilath Jeshurun (New
York, N.Y.) 5. New York (N.Y.)—Biography. I. Title.
    BM755.L645M43 2008
    296.8'32092—dc22
    [B]
                                                    2008020636




                        Published by
            KTAV Publishing House, Inc.
                  930 Newark Avenue
                  Jersey City, NJ 07306
              Email: orders@ktav.com
                     www.ktav.com
                    (201) 963-9524
                  Fax (201) 963-0102

Dedicated to the memory of
Rabbi Joseph H. and Gertrude Lookstein

# Table of Contents

# ACKNOWLEDGMENTS

This biographical essay is part of a larger project commemorating Rabbi Haskel Lookstein's fiftieth year in the pulpit of Kehilath Jeshurun. I am grateful to the KJ committee overseeing the project, Jay K. R. Lunzer, Dr. Jeffrey Gurock, Dr. Roy Feldman, Rabbi Joshua Cypess, Dr. Gilbert Kahn, Rabbi Jeffrey Kobrin, Lawrence A. Kobrin, Rabbi Joshua Lookstein, Rabbi Adam Mintz, Rabbi Meir Soloveichick, Surie R. Sugerman, Adele Tauber, and Rabbi Elie Weinstock, for their support, encouragement, and input. Jay Lunzer's leadership of the project, and Jeffrey Gurock's careful analysis of several drafts of this manuscript, are most deeply appreciated by this author.

Numerous individuals kindly made themselves available for interviews, especially Rabbi Haskel and Audrey Lookstein, and their children Mindy, Debbie, Shira, and Joshua. I am grateful for their cooperation. Thanks, too, to the staff at the Kehilath Jeshurun office, for facilitating my research in the synagogue's voluminous files.

Finally, a special thanks to KTAV Publishing House vice president Bernard Scharfstein and managing editor Adam Bengal for expertly shepherding the manuscript through the publication process despite the pressures of an extremely tight production schedule.

Rafael Medoff
May 2008

# INTRODUCTION

Biography—the venture of trying to capture on paper the story of someone else's life—is often a risky enterprise, and all the more risky when the life in question is still being lived. To the usual hazards of not telling at least all that is significant must be added both the distinct possibility that some event will overtake what is already recorded, and the certainty that the subject will be present to offer his own view, which is bound to differ from his biographer's. However, when one looks at the title and the ten chapter headings in Rafael Medoff's fascinating account of Rabbi Haskel Lookstein's journey among us, what becomes clear is that whatever disadvantage may lurk in those mundane hazards is far outweighed by the importance of having this volume, and particularly of having it while Rabbi Lookstein continues to lead and to teach us.

The ten chapter headings—beginning with "The Student" and ending with "The Teacher"—describe aspects of Rabbi Lookstein's life that are ongoing. Although many people lead lives sequentially, with one chapter ending and another beginning, sometimes with indeterminate gaps between, none of the chapters in this book, even as they may describe particular events and activities that are in the past, has an end. Pick any at random—"The Scholar" or "The Activist" or "Women's Issues" or "The Zionist"—and you will call to mind events and concerns that are ongoing in Rabbi Lookstein's life. The key lies in the title: *Rav Chesed.* These chapters are facets of a person whose motivating and defining force is chesed. This is a volume that is important not only to help us to understand a person who is among us, but also thereby to improve the lives of those around us, k'lal yisrael, and ourselves. Its force is enhanced by the happy fact that if there is this or that point that we don't get, we have the subject to teach it to us, by explanation if necessary but in any event by example. This is a good read insofar as it tells us about some of Rabbi Lookstein's achievements; it is an important one insofar as it reminds us of our own unrealized potential.

Michael B. Mukasey[1]
May 2008

[1] Mr. Mukasey is a member of Congregation Kehilath Jeshurun and a former student of Rabbi Lookstein at Ramaz School. He has served since November 2007 as the Attorney General of the United States.

# About the Author

*Dr. Rafael Medoff is founding director of The David S. Wyman Institute for Holocaust Studies, which focuses on America's response to Nazism and the Holocaust [www.WymanInstitute.org]. He is the author of eight books about American Jewish history, Zionism, and the Holocaust, as well as essays for the* Encyclopedia Judaica *and numerous other reference volumes. Dr. Medoff has served as associate editor of the scholarly journal* American Jewish History *and has taught Jewish history at Ohio State University, SUNY-Purchase, and elsewhere.*

# I. THE STUDENT

On a crisp Monday morning in early September 1937, Rabbi Joseph H. Lookstein led his five year old son, Haskel, into a classroom in the fledgling Ramaz elementary school on East 85th Street, next door to its sponsor, Congregation Kehilath Jeshurun. The inauguration of the school launched a major new attempt to combine Orthodoxy and modernity in a Manhattan neighborhood that few considered fertile ground for Jewish religious observance. The experiment would ultimately succeed far beyond its sponsors' expectations. Under the leadership of Rabbi Lookstein, and later of his son, Ramaz would come to be recognized as one of the most influential Jewish day schools in the United States, Kehilath Jeshurun would emerge as one of America's most important synagogues, and the Upper East Side would blossom into a thriving center of Jewish life. Nurturing a local community while at the same time influencing the entire American Jewish community, the Looksteins would make their mark with an innovative blend of traditional observance, respect for modernity, social activism, tolerance, and personal compassion.

\* \* \*

Joseph H. Lookstein first came to Kehilath Jeshurun in 1923, as assistant rabbi under the renowned sage Rabbi Moses Margolies, better known by the acronym RaMaZ. Three years later he married Margolies's granddaughter, Gertrude Schlang, and when their daughter Nathalie reached the age of five, in 1932, he began exploring the possibility of establishing a day school on the Upper East Side. The 1930s were hardly an auspicious time to establish a new Jewish school, especially in an area with a small Jewish presence such as the Yorkville section of Upper Manhattan, where Kehilath Jeshurun was situated. The Great Depression drastically reduced the pool of potential donors, and the neighborhood was best known for pro-Nazi rallies by the German-American Bund. By 1937, when Rabbi Lookstein's son Haskel turned five and was ready to enter first grade, the rabbi was determined to launch a Jewish elementary school, regardless of these obstacles.[1]

The neighborhood and the national economy were not the only hindrances to his plan. It was also a period of intense turmoil for American Judaism. Many Jewish immigrants chose to leave behind their old-world religious observances and assimilate into American society. Only a small minority clung to the traditional lifestyle they had known in Europe. Rabbi Lookstein was among those who sought a middle ground between these two extremes, as he worked to build a community that would remain loyal to tradition while at the same time embracing the best of modern American life.

At a meeting of the KJ board of trustees in 1937, he presented his vision of an institution that would integrate Judaic learning with secular studies, embodying the spirit of the modern, Americanized Orthodoxy to which they subscribed. Such a school was "an imperative necessity for an entire generation of growing young people," he argued. Most of the approximately fifteen Orthodox day schools in New York City were widely perceived as "ghetto schools." They were situated "in underprivileged neighborhoods and were considered as suited for poor underprivileged children." The children of more successful, native-born American Orthodox Jews did not regard such schools as "congenial or acceptable." Judaic studies were taught in Yiddish, by teachers who did not understand "the modern American Jewish children," while secular studies were relegated to the end of the ten-hour school day, when "tired teachers were expected to teach tired children."[2]

The school Rabbi Lookstein proposed to build would be unique in two important respects. First, it would bring to the Upper East Side a type of day school unknown to that area and barely represented elsewhere in New York City: a modern Orthodox alternative to, on the one hand, a traditional *cheder* that would leave their children ill equipped to succeed in the outside world, and, on the other hand, a public school that would leave the youngsters bereft of Jewish knowledge. Ramaz would offer the best of both worlds. Second, it would consciously seek to recruit students from less religiously observant families. Doing this was a virtual necessity given the small size of the neighborhood's Orthodox community, but it also created an unusual opportunity to influence Jewish families to become more observant.

R. Joseph's proposal met with some skepticism among KJ board members. Some regarded day schools as "too parochial," preferring that Jewish children be sent to public schools and receive a limited supplementary Judaic education. Others doubted that the synagogue could shoulder the financial burden of a new school, which would inevitably run a deficit at least in its early years.

Rabbi Lookstein would not yield. He informed the board that if Kehilath Jeshurun were unwilling to take on the project, he would resign and find another synagogue that would implement his vision. The stalemate was resolved when Max J. Etra, a prominent attorney and lay leader in the congregation, pledged to cover the first year's deficit, which the rabbi estimated would be $5,000.[3]

Lookstein named the school after Rabbi Margolies, a renowned scholar from Vilna whose intellectual feats included studying the complete Talmud each year. Significantly, the RaMaZ was also known for his substantial involvement in community affairs. A famous photograph shows Rabbi Margolies participating in the founding meeting of the American Jewish Joint Distribution Committee, the overseas relief agency run primarily by non-Orthodox Jews. His willingness to work side by side with Jews of other backgrounds and differing levels of religious observance was emblematic of a spirit of tolerance for which his grandson and great-grandson would become well known.[4]

In 1932, shortly after his son was born, Rabbi Joseph Lookstein visited the RaMaZ to receive a blessing. As the story goes, Rabbi Margolies had just read about the passing of Rabbi Hatzkel [Yehezkel] Kalischer, a distinguished scholar with whom RaMaZ had been close. He suggested to Rabbi Lookstein that the baby be named Hatzkel, "so he will grow up to be like Reb Hatzkel." Lookstein was pleased with the idea, regarding it as a harbinger of success for his son, but he worried that his wife and mother would be less than thrilled "about naming him after some Polish rabbi" instead of a relative. They conspired to present the name as connected to RaMaZ's father and uncle, both of whom were named Yechezkel. Gertrude Lookstein accepted the proposal but planned to also give him Charles as his English name, to which Rabbi Lookstein objected on the grounds that the boy, named for a renowned rabbi, would undoubtedly be called "Chuck." Their compromise solution was to use the slightly Americanized "Haskel," although the future Rabbi Lookstein was immediately nicknamed "Hack" or "Hacky" by family and friends alike.

As a child, Haskel exhibited musical ability which he attributed to two influences. One was his maternal grandfather, Isidore Schlang, a devout "shul yid" who was always the first to come to morning minyan and the last to leave, reciting his prayers slowly and punctiliously. When Haskel led the service, his grandfather would remind him of the importance of pronouncing every word—"Hacky, say woids!" he would implore him. Schlang's passion for Shabbat *zmirot* made a strong impression on young Haskel, who subsequently adopted his grandfather's tune for *birkat ha-mazon* [grace after meals], as would his children and grandchildren.[5]

An equally profound influence on Haskel was Joseph E. Adler, who began working at Kehilath Jeshurun in 1933 as sexton, Torah reader, and second *chazan*. Adler, who would later gain renown in the kosher food industry for Mrs. Adler's Gefilte Fish [based on his wife's recipe], was deeply involved in community affairs and worked closely with Rabbi Joseph Lookstein in building the synagogue and the school. He was Haskel's model for Torah reading and as *shaliach tzibur* [leader of the communal prayer service], and Adler's *nusach* became Haskel's. "I just loved to listen to him," he recalled. "My davening is his davening."[6]

After Haskel turned thirteen, Adler would call on him to read *maftir*, without advance notice, if the scheduled person did not show up. "I was able to read the *haftorah* without preparation simply because I loved it," he noted. "When you enjoy something so much, you get good at it." The text commonly used in those days was a nineteenth-century edition by Isaac Leeser, which had the esoteric textual variations and corrections at the bottom of the page rather than in the text itself as in contemporary versions. Thus Haskel needed to check those variations at the bottom of the page during the *misheberach*. When he concluded the reading, Adler, sitting at the back of the *bima*, instead of complimenting his protégé, would inevitably point out to Haskel some obscure error he had made. Haskel considered this the ultimate compliment, realizing that his consummate mentor expected from him nothing less than absolute perfection.[7]

Rabbi Lookstein has described Torah reading and leading the davening as "my biggest *yetzer hara*." A small part of him would have preferred to follow in the footsteps of Joseph Adler rather than of his father, Joseph Lookstein, although ultimately he would come to derive satisfaction from the realization that his davening in fact supplemented his rabbinical leadership. Making the prayers meaningful helped inspire congregants to feel more connected to the synagogue and the community, an ingredient crucial to the success of a rabbi's mission. Over the years, he had the opportunity to indulge himself on the few Shabbatot when the *chazan* was absent, and, most notably, during the High Holidays. From his father and maternal grandfather, Rabbi Haskel Lookstein learned the importance of "emphasizing every word, and putting feeling into every word." His style left a strong impression on his congregants. A Ramaz alumnus who attended only one Yom Kippur service at KJ, twenty-five years later still vividly remembered the rabbi leading *shacharit* and *ne'ila*, "with a powerful but musical voice, filled with emotion and concentration, leaving behind his day-to-day rabbinic persona and becoming a true *eved Hashem* [servant of God].'"[8]

"Some day, I am sure, my voice will begin to crack and waver, and I will have to very reluctantly accept the fact that I can do only *ne'ila* but not *shacharit*," he conceded. "Somebody, perhaps my wife, will find a gentle way to alert me that the time has come. I won't be happy about it, but it's inevitable."[9] In the meantime, however, the KJ-Ramaz community made clear its appreciation for his singing. R. Haskel's solo rendition of the song "Chazak, Chazak," performed according to the tune and style of noted Jewish singer Avraham Fried, has been a highlight of the Ramaz Upper School's annual banquet since 1999. The congregation's celebration of R. Haskel's seventieth birthday, in 2002, with a gala dinner at the Marriott Hotel, included a video clip of him singing that song. It took little coaxing to convince the rabbi to do a live version on stage at the birthday event, where he was joined by a surprise guest—Avraham Fried himself.[10]

Haskel grew up in a family that was close-knit, with a full-time, stay-at-home mother and a father to whom he felt close despite the elder Rabbi Lookstein's hectic professional life as spiritual leader of KJ and principal of Ramaz. Gertrude Lookstein managed an equally busy life as mother, wife, and rebbitzen. She founded and led the KJ Sisterhood; instructed the shul's young women in caring for *shiva* houses, visiting the sick, and performing other social mitzvahs; and hosted a constant stream of Shabbat and Yom Tov guests. "We had open house in our home, visitors for dinner Friday night and Shabbos lunch and every holiday," she recalled. "Both my husband and I enjoyed it. And the people enjoyed it. We never sat down alone."[11]

Haskel looked up to his older sister, Nathalie, whom he regarded as "a wonderful role model but a tough act to follow—she rarely got less than an 'A' in anything." He remembered attending her graduation ceremony [from Hunter High School; Ramaz did not exist when she began school], at which Nathalie and another Jewish girl received seventeen of the eighteen scholastic awards, and wondering if he would earn even one award in his high school class. Nathalie would go on to earn a Ph. D. in sociology and lead a distinguished academic career at Barnard College and Stern College.

Haskel's years at Ramaz were not always a smooth ride. When he reached eighth grade, he "hit a wall," as he later put it, engaging in frequent mischief that caused his teachers and parents considerable aggravation. R. Haskel would later attribute this difficult period to the pressure of fellow students targeting "the principal's son," together with his anxiety over his height. He was four foot five at the time of his bar mitzvah in March 1945 and needed to stand on a platform in order to read from the Torah. "But, thank God, I grew eleven inches in the next two years," he recalled.[12]

Some of the eighth-grade troublemaking was comical. If a student was caught talking while their Hebrew teacher that year, Morris Nieman, was writing on the board, "Nieman would suddenly pivot like a baseball pitcher throwing to second base to pick off a runner—only he would throw his eraser at the student. And he had good aim." R. Haskel recalled the day when Nieman wheeled and hurled the eraser at him, assuming that he was, as usual, the culprit. But with his fast reflexes, Haskel flipped up his desk in time to cause the eraser to ricochet and strike the guilty student, Peppy Friedberg [later chairman of Loews Entertainment Corporation]. Other episodes were less amusing. One teacher, Samuel Goodside, would make a notation in his roll book next to a student's name each time that student engaged in unusually bad behavior. Aside from Haskel, the worst student in that eighth-grade class racked up six notations; Haskel had twenty-five. After the twenty-fifth, some horseplay in which a fellow student accidentally injured Haskel, R. Joseph gave his son "a tongue-lashing that I can remember clearly, even though it's sixty-two years later. ... It was a very sobering event in my life."

For Haskel, the incident was a turning point. By the time he began ninth grade, he had become a serious and devoted student. Rabbi Nachum Bronznick, whose first full-time teaching position, at Ramaz, fortunately coincided with the year Haskel was in ninth grade and therefore took his class, later recalled his anxiety at the prospect of having the principal's son as one of his pupils. "To my great relief, however, I discovered soon enough that I had nothing to be uneasy about," he noted. "This student, happily, did not show any sign that he was expecting any special treatment. He acted and behaved as a true and sincere young mensch in every respect." Rabbi Bronznick noted that while it was common for students to approach him after an exam was returned and argue for additional points, Haskel came to him after a particular test, saying, "I am not coming to argue why I didn't get credit for this particular answer, but I want to understand what is wrong with it, and what is the correct answer." The incident convinced the teacher that this pupil "was destined to become a person with many great achievements to his credit, as he indeed became."[13]

Haskel excelled throughout his remaining high school years, finishing as the second highest student in his class. In retrospect, that rough patch in eighth grade offered him a valuable lesson:

> As a result of that experience, when I look at students whom the educational system is ready to give up on, I have an entirely different perspective. I know that students can change. Sometimes the kid who is most out of line can get back in line and straighten himself out. What happened to me gave me a lot of empathy for kids in junior high school, who can go through a difficult time before turning out very well. When I run into such students, I often tell them, and their parents, about my own experience, to help them realize that there's hope.[14]

Haskel's ten summers at Camp Massad, beginning in 1945, included a number of formative experiences. The Hebrew-language camp, run by Shlomo and Rivka Shulsinger, was situated in Tannersville, Pennsylvania, in the Pocono Mountains. There Haskel exhibited a prowess at basketball, tennis, and softball that would last long after his camp years were over. With Lookstein as its star pitcher, the younger campers' softball team [13 year-olds] defeated not only their peers but the older division as well, and the year Haskel turned 15, his team beat the teams of counselors and waiters as well. His enthusiasm for basketball carried over into the school year, when as captain of the team in his senior year—"it was me, at five foot three, with four boys who were six feet or taller"—he averaged more than ten points per game. Those experiences, together with occasional teenage forays to the Polo Grounds with his father to watch the New York Giants, nurtured Haskel's lifelong passion for professional sports. Six decades later he would describe as one of the highlights of his life the day in 2006 that KJ members arranged for him to throw out the ceremonial first pitch at a New York Mets game. Surrounded by KJers with "Lookstein Puts the RBI in Rabbi" t-shirts, R. Haskel threw a strike. When the Mets fell behind in the first inning, a fan sitting near R. Haskel and his friends shouted, "Hey rabbi, maybe you should get back out there and pitch!"[15]

Haskel made a quick transition from ordinary camper to a leader-in-training in the summer of 1947, when the counselor in charge of tefillah for the older campers seven days a week asked 15-year-old Haskel if he would supervise the weekday minyan. Haskel felt a special affinity for davening and accepted the offer without hesitation. "I taught the boys how to daven correctly, practicing the nusach with everyone out loud," he recalled. "At the time, I didn't realize what a major turning point it was, but looking back now, I realize that was the point where I started becoming interested in Jewish education and the rabbinate as a possible career." For the rest of the summers while he was in high school, and all through his college years, Haskel continued to serve as the *rosh tefillah* for the campers at Massad.[16]

Michael Mukasey, who in 2007 became Attorney General of the United States, was a camper in Massad's "Deganyia" division of older campers, over which counselor Haskel presided one summer. "He had everyone's respect in part because he could do everything we thought was important—which is to say he could hit, pitch, field, take a jump shot, get his first serve in, and hit a backhand—and do it better than we could," and in part because of his "fine and gentle demeanor, the kind that makes people lean forward to listen when he speaks." Mukasey remembered Haskel "unobtrusively looking in on even the most spontaneous and unorganized of activities, just to make sure that everyone was included [and that we were all speaking Hebrew]." But most of all, he remembered Haskel as "the only person I have ever seen participate in a water fight and maintain his dignity."[17]

Haskel graduated from Ramaz in the spring of 1949, as valedictorian of his class and president of the student government. He entered Columbia University that fall. He was, his father later noted with considerable pride, "the first student of Ramaz to have gained admission to Columbia and, therefore, the one who blazed a trail which was followed at Columbia and Barnard by a generation of Ramaz graduates." The fact that a significant percentage of Ramaz graduates attend Ivy League colleges became more than a badge of pride for Ramaz. It demonstrated the school's educational quality and also made a broader statement about the ability of modern Orthodox Jews to reach the highest echelons of American society. In effect, it helped validate one of the central contentions of the Centrist Orthodoxy that the Looksteins so passionately advocated.

Uncertain as to his career direction, Haskel enrolled in a wide range of courses at Columbia. Friends and relatives, his father included, assumed that in view of his oratorical and intellectual skills, Haskel would become an attorney; in fact, however, Haskel had no interest in doing so. Finally, late in his junior year, he sought his father's counsel in choosing a career path.

> "In one more year I will graduate from Columbia as an educated bum," I told him. My father was not much interested in self-pity. He pressed me to name the field that interested me most. I said Jewish education, recalling how, at Massad, I had developed an interest in other people's religious behavior and ways in which I could help them. "Well," he said, "do you want to be a teacher or do you want to someday be principal of the school?" In our conversations, my father often criticized me but he also had an insightful way of clarifying issues and choices.[18]

Interestingly, Rabbi Lookstein had never spoken to his son about becoming a rabbi, although in retrospect Haskel assumed that some people in the congregation did harbor expectations that he would follow in his father's footsteps. R. Joseph told his son that if his goal was "to be a Jewish educator," then he had to "become educated Jewishly." It would not suffice to take courses in education—"if that is all you do, you'll become a plumber in Jewish education." The way to do it, he advised, was "after finishing your B.A. at Columbia College, enroll at Yeshiva University, attain rabbinical ordination, and then go into Jewish education." Haskel later speculated that his father may have had an unstated agenda, urging his son to pursue *smicha* ostensibly for a career in education but quietly hoping it would lead him down the path to the rabbinate.

Haskel decided to test the waters. Never having studied gemara for long periods of time, he wanted to be sure he was capable and enjoyed it sufficiently before making a multiyear commitment. For six weeks in the summer of 1952 [the end of his junior year at Columbia] he traveled each day to Crown Heights to study gemara with Rabbi Norman Lamm, Joseph Lookstein's rabbinic assistant at KJ. "My pupil was alert, quick, and took to the material—which could be quite abstruse—very readily," Rabbi Lamm recalled. "His native intelligence helped him overcome the inertia and listlessness urged on us by the summer heat." From Haskel's perspective, too, the experiment was a success; he concluded that he was both able and interested, so much so that he opted to complete his final courses at Columbia in the fall of 1952 in order to begin his studies at Yeshiva University in the spring of 1953, forgoing his final semester at college.[19]

Haskel being accustomed to the quiet, dignified atmosphere of Columbia's Butler Library ["If you whispered, you would be expelled," he joked], the scene he encountered when he entered the Y.U. beis midrash for the first time was something of a culture shock. "When I heard the level of noise, I thought to myself, 'How can anyone study with such a cacophony of voices?' People were yelling, wrestling with each other over a *tosefos*, hurling arguments back and forth in a way that was completely new to me."

His years at the Rabbi Isaac Elchanan Theological Seminary, Yeshiva University's rabbinical school, [RIETS] exposed Haskel to some of the leading lights of contemporary Orthodox scholarship. In his first year he learned in the highest-level shiur of Samuel Sar, dean of students, while also learning privately with Rabbi Joseph Weiss, a rosh yeshiva, whom Haskel soon came to regard as his first "rebbe." The following year he studied Tractate Sanhedrin with Rabbi Avigdor Cyperstein. That year he also began a limited but formal connection to Ramaz by tutoring eighth graders for their bar mitzvahs.[20]

From there he moved up to the gemara shiur of Rabbi Joseph B. Soloveitchik. "I was very fortunate," he recalled. "He admitted me to the shiur even though I had much less background in serious Talmud study than the boys who had gone to Yeshiva College as undergraduates. But he evidently felt I had enough ability and potential to succeed, and so his approach toward me became, as he put it, 'stuff him like an ox.'"

Haskel's participation in Rabbi Soloveitchik's shiur created an unexpected dilemma. He had already completed two and a half years of study at Y.U. at that point, meaning he could complete his remaining requirements with other instructors and graduate in two more years. But as fate would have it, the Rav was just then inaugurating a special three- year study plan for rabbinical students, which involved learning Talmud and Shulchan Aruch together, with him. Haskel was torn between continuing on his path to graduate in two years or switching to the Rav's multiyear program and considerably delaying his graduation. Dean Sar provided the advice that "completely changed and informed my life," as Rabbi Lookstein later put it: "Spending an extra year in Y.U. won't reduce your life expectancy—but being able to spend four years learning with the Rav could make all the difference in the world." Rabbi Lookstein recalled:

No one has ever given me better advice than that. Intellectually, religiously, and philosophically, the Rav was the greatest influence on my life. He was so influential that when I read his book, *Ish Ha-Halacha*, I was astonished at how much he was in tune with my whole worldview. Then, of course, I realized that it was the other way around—that after so many years of exposure to him, I had so internalized his teachings, it looked to me like *he* was speaking *my* language—rather than me thinking some of his thoughts.[21]

## NOTES

[1] Rafael Medoff interview with Rabbi Haskel Lookstein [hereafter cited as RHL interview], 10 July 2007.

[2] Rabbi Joseph H. Lookstein, "Ramaz at Forty—A Sentimental History," undated [1977] [New York: Kehilath Jeshurun, 1977], pp. 3–4.

[3] RHL interview, 10 July 2007.

[4] Rabbi Margolies's willingness to work with non-Orthodox Jews is explored in Jeffrey S. Gurock, *American Jewish Orthodoxy in Historical Perspective* [Hoboken, N.J.: Ktav, 1996], pp. 19–23.

[5] Ibid.

[6] Ibid.

[7] Ibid.

[8] Ibid.; Francesca Lunzer Kritz interview with Rafael Medoff, 2 December 2007.

[9] RHL interview,10 July 2007.

[10] RHL interview, 12 February 2008.

[11] "Oral History," *Kehilath Jeshurun Bulletin* [hereafter KJB], December 1997, p.12.

[12] RHL interview, 10 July 2007.

[13] Nachum Bronznick memoir in *Ner L'Echad Ner L'Meah: Rabbi Haskel Lookstein* [New York: Kehilath Jeshurun,1998].

[14] RHL interview, 10 July 2007.

[15] RHL interview, 12 February 2008.

[16] RHL interview, 10 July 2007; Dr. Shlomo Shulsinger-Shar Yashuv memoir in Adele Tauber, ed., *Haskel Lookstein: Teacher, Preacher and Leader* [New York: Kehilath Jeshurun, 1983] [hereafter *Teacher,Preacher*], p.14.

[17] Michael Mukasey memoir in *Teacher, Preacher*, p. 14.

[18] RHL interview, 10 July 2007.

[19] Ibid.; Dr. Norman Lamm, "Unintended Consequence," in *Teacher, Preacher*, p. 24.

[20] RHL interview, 10 July 2007.

[21] RHL interview, 25 July 2007.

## II. THE RABBI

In the spring of 1958, five and a half years after he began his studies at RIETS, Haskel Lookstein received his rabbinical ordination. He had been one of the top students in the Rav's *shiur*, focusing almost all his time on his studies there. The only exception had been for the limited time he devoted to teaching the bar mitzvah and cantillation classes at Ramaz, something he had taken on after Joseph Adler departed for the gefilte fish business. It was a job that had become a labor of love for Haskel; teaching the boys how to *layn* [read from the Torah] and daven was actually what he enjoyed most, and there was an important practical achievement as well: "For five and a half years I developed boys who were really proficient at reading the Torah—not just reading their bar mitzvah portion, but giving them the skills for a lifetime of *layning.*"

R. Joseph, however, felt strongly that bar mitzvah tutoring was no longer an appropriate task now that Haskel had achieved ordination. In his view, that was a job better left to a rabbinical student. Haskel reluctantly agreed to give it up.

But there is an exception to every rule, and in the late spring of 1958, after Haskel's final year at RIETS, a prominent lay leader at KJ, Alexander Gross, asked him to tutor his son Steven for his bar mitzvah [to be held in June 1959]. "I told him I knew that Steven was a good student," he recalled, "and I would love to teach him, but my father had instructed me not to do any more bar mitzvah tutoring, especially in view of the possibility that I would become assistant rabbi at KJ." Gross was insistent. "Of course your father is right," he said. "But my Stevenyu!" Haskel made an exception, and never regretted it. Gross grew up to become an important leader in the Jewish community, chairman of the board of Ramaz, and a major force behind the building of the Ramaz middle school and other projects. "And he can still read a flawless *haftorah*," Rabbi Haskel noted with pride.[1]

During his final year at RIETS, Haskel, like all *s̀micha* students, met with Victor Geller, director of Y.U.'s Office of Rabbinic Placement. As is customary, he was offered two possible positions. "One was in Detroit and I didn't want to go there, because I naively believed there were few single Jewish girls there," he recalled. "I was the most provincial person you ever saw—I had lived my whole life between 84th and 86th Streets, and Lexington and Madison Avenues. I could not imagine viable Jewish communal life existed as far away as Detroit." The second possible pulpit was for a Sephardic shul that was being developed in Cedarhurst, Long Island. "I was not ready to become a Sephardic rabbi either."[2]

Dissatisfied with those prospects, Haskel approached his father about the possibility of a position at KJ. "Both my son and I were excited about the idea but we entertained serious reservations as well," according to R. Joseph's account. "It is never easy for a father and son to work together in the same profession and under the same roof. In the rabbinate it is almost unheard of." Moreover, Haskel recognized that it would have been better if he had served his first pulpit in some other congregation, where he could gain some experience and establish a record of institutional success, before coming to KJ. But given the circumstances, he thought KJ might work. Victor Geller was less than encouraging: "Haskel, you could do it, but you have to understand what you're getting into," he said, and then offered a baseball analogy that the sports-loving young rabbi could readily appreciate: "It's like the seventh game of the World Series, the last of the ninth inning, the score is tied, the bases are loaded, there are no outs and the count is 3 and 0. And you are summoned from the bullpen. It's possible to get out without a run scoring. But you can't make a single mistake." Haskel's interpretation: it's difficult but feasible. Geller laughed when he recalled the story many years later; he was, in fact, trying to warn him against taking the job.[3]

Kehilath Jeshurun's lay leaders were not of one mind regarding the possibility of Haskel becoming assistant rabbi at that time. Max Etra, who had been president of the synagogue since 1940, felt strongly that Haskel should first obtain experience in a different community prior to working at KJ. But a group of supporters, led by Alexander Gross, Oscar Perlberger, and Yeshiva University president Dr. Samuel Belkin, pressed ahead with a board of trustees meeting, in Rabbi Joseph Lookstein's home, to decide the matter.[4]

The episode highlights R. Joseph's unusually powerful position. In most synagogues the rabbi is an employee who does not typically attend board meetings, much less play a significant role in its decisions. Joseph Lookstein, by contrast, completely involved himself in the governance of the synagogue and the school. He took part in board meetings and, although they did not normally take place in the rabbi's home, none of the board members looked askance at the fact that the meeting concerning R. Haskel's status was held there, even though that very fact could be seen as influencing the board's decision. Whatever the private qualms of the board members about hiring R. Haskel at that time, it is hard to imagine them defying their revered rabbi in his own living room. Sure enough, whatever opposition might have existed had melted by the time Dr. Belkin made the nomination. "Then, it is reported, something most unusual occurred," according to the KJ newsletter. "Everyone among those present seconded the nomination." Two weeks later R. Haskel was formally installed as assistant rabbi and "accepted the mantle of his new post with dignity," the newsletter reported.[5]

R. Haskel's transition from rabbinical student to assistant rabbi was facilitated by two key relationships. One was with Dr. Belkin, who happened to sit in the front row at KJ, immediately adjacent to R. Haskel. "Whenever I delivered a sermon, as I returned to my seat, he would spring to his feet, his hand extended, and give me a big "*yasher koach*"—even if the sermon wasn't so great," R. Haskel remembered. "It was indicative of the fact that he was, beneath his reserved exterior, a warm, gracious, and extremely kind man."

The other important relationship was with the Rav, Rabbi Joseph Soloveitchik. Because of his stature as a scholar and leader, some of his students and admirers hesitated to approach him personally. R. Haskel, however, established a closer than usual talmid–rebbe rapport with him early on and always felt comfortable consulting with him about matters large and small. In an address in the main synagogue on the occasion of the 100th anniversary of Kehilath Jeshurun, Rabbi Soloveitchik, after strongly praising Rabbi Joseph Lookstein, turned to R. Haskel, sitting in the front row, and said, "Chatzkel, do you want me to say something about you too?" ["I would have liked to fall through a trap door at that moment," R. Haskel later mused.] He then remarked, "Your father, I respect. You, I love."[6]

On one occasion, during a shiur after the Rav had developed an extensive analytic argument about a certain subject in the Talmud, Haskel noticed what he perceived to be a contradiction between the Rav's argument and a point the Rav had made during a shiur some months earlier. "Rebbe," he asked, "how does this fit with the analysis that we developed some months ago?" The Rav, his eyes wide with surprise, thought for a moment and then said to the class: "You are right, I am wrong. Do you hear, students? Lookstein is correct, I am incorrect. I'll have to go home and relearn the entire subject and present it again tomorrow."[7]

The detailed memoranda of his conversations with the Rav in the early 1980s, which Rabbi Lookstein composed for his private reference, indicate that he routinely consulted the Rav on a range of issues, from the minutiae of traditional ritual observances to the unique concerns of the modern era. One session in early 1982 included discussions about women dancing with a sefer Torah on Simchat Torah, the use of prenuptial agreements to ameliorate the agunah problem, requirements for conversion, the permissibility of spelling out the word "God," and the reheating of foods on Shabbat. Another, in the autumn of 1984, addressed such issues as aborting a Tay Sachs pregnancy, calling a Reform rabbi to the Torah in an Orthodox synagogue, and what kind of public transgressions would disqualify someone from serving as a witness at a Jewish wedding.[8]

The topics raised in the conversations between R. Lookstein and R. Soloveitchik point to the difficulties facing rabbis in the modern era, the changing role of the rabbi in his synagogue and community, and the unique problems confronting modern Orthodoxy in navigating between old-world-style Judaism and the lures of American society. From the moment he assumed the position of assistant rabbi at Kehilath Jeshurun, Haskel Lookstein became acutely aware of these challenges.

The examples set by his great-grandfather, and especially, his father, offered R. Haskel additional guidance as he embarked on his new position. The historians Adam Ferziger and Jeffrey Gurock have pointed out that although the RaMaZ was in many respects a "rabbi from the old school," some of his actions belied that stereotype, including his support for Zionism, his willingness to work with non-Orthodox rabbis in Jewish organizational functions, and his invitation to Hebrew University chancellor Judah Magnes to speak at KJ on Yom Kippur eve despite Magnes's affiliation with Reform Judaism.[9] Rabbi Joseph Lookstein went considerably further, shaping and promoting Americanized Orthodoxy not as a grudging concession to modern pressures—as some of his colleagues in the Orthodox rabbinate regarded it—but as an approach that stood on its own as a comprehensive ideology.

When R. Joseph became assistant rabbi at KJ back in 1923, Orthodox synagogue life in Manhattan had not been at all to his liking. Contemporary critics described the typical Lower East Side synagogue of that era as small, overcrowded, unkempt, and even "un-American"—that is, out of step with modern, American houses of worship.[10] KJ was just beginning to attract "self-consciously, upwardly mobile immigrants [for whom] the indecorous and informal downtown synagogue served as an uncomfortable reminder of their immigrant origins and of their un-Americanized selves," the historian Jenna Joselit has pointed out. R. Joseph made it one of his priorities to improve KJ's physical appearance. He believed that with the right presentation, Orthodoxy could constitute a viable alternative to Reform and Conservative Judaism on the Upper East Side. He went so far as to "personally inspect the building from top to bottom, making sure that the bathrooms were clean, the brass finishings of the sanctuary polished, and its prayer books untattered and regularly dusted."[11]

Prayer services adhered to Orthodox liturgy but were conducted in as orderly and dignified a manner as possible. "Our intention," Rabbi Lookstein later recalled, "was to conduct the kind of public worship that would be as dignified as the most Reform and as pious as the worship in a '*shteibbel.*'"[12] A small portion of the services were even conducted in English, a practice not forbidden by Jewish law but unusual in an Orthodox synagogue. "From personal experience, I have seen the welcome thrill on the faces of worshipers when, for example, during a Yizkor service an English psalm or prayer is read," he wrote. "I am convinced that a slight concession in this regard might keep within the folds of Orthodoxy a multitude who might otherwise desert us."[13]

Throughout his career, R. Joseph closely scrutinized his congregants' behavior to ensure appropriate comportment. As late as 1976, near the end of his tenure at KJ, he was admonishing the congregation for its "overindulgence in handshaking" after someone was called to the Torah. "The handshaking syndrome has become almost a compulsive act," he wrote in an appeal in the KJ newsletter. "People have been seen to walk from a far end of the synagogue in order to shake the hand and congratulate someone who had an aliyah or any other honor. It is utterly unnecessary to do that and, moreover, it is a disturbing practice and interferes with the dignity and the order of public worship." He proposed that "a friendly and dignified nod of the head" would constitute a more appropriate gesture.[14]

In R. Joseph's view, personal attire too constituted an integral part of congregational dignity. The *KJ Bulletin* often featured his appeals for appropriate dress. A typical remonstrance, appearing in the newsletter in 1965, pointed out that when one observes "devotees of other faiths going to their respective places of worship," the men "wear dark clothes and black shoes" and "the women invariably are dressed becomingly but in modesty." KJ members should do no less, R. Joseph admonished: "A dark suit and black shoes—not tan, not loafers—should be the standard for men," and "as for the ladies, they will understand what modesty in dress is."[15]

For all his emphasis on order and decorum, R. Joseph seems to have harbored a certain limited fondness for the exuberance that character-izes Chassidic worship. While his idea of appropriate behavior during services was quite different from what would be found in a Chassidic *shteibel*, he proudly noted in the KJ newsletter in 1965 that "Chassidic spirit is a rare phenomenon in Yorkville but on Simchat Torah it is experienced in full in our synagogue."[16] Likewise, his description of a teenagers' Shabbaton at KJ that year expressed pleasure that the youths "sang Chassidic songs and danced with a fervor not usually associated with groups in our neighborhood."[17]

The years that Joseph Lookstein occupied the KJ pulpit were a peri-od of struggle and change for Orthodox Judaism in America, and R. Joseph was often on the front lines. The pressures of integrating into American life had pushed many Jewish immigrants and children of immigrants to leave Orthodoxy for Conservative Judaism. In the late 1930s, when R. Joseph succeeded the RaMaZ as senior rabbi at KJ, Orthodoxy was numerically the largest of American Judaism's denom-inations. But many of its adherents practiced what Jeffrey Gurock has characterized as "inconsistent Orthodoxy"; that is, they were lax in their personal religious observance, although they chose to be mem-bers of an Orthodox synagogue.[18] On the infrequent occasions when they took part in synagogue life—typically on the High Holidays—they felt more comfortable doing so in an Orthodox setting. Rabbi Lookstein built KJ in the 1940s and 1950s by actively competing for the support of these inconsistent Orthodox. Making KJ physically attractive helped win the affections of aesthetic-minded, upwardly mobile, and religiously casual Upper East Siders.

In the 1950s and 1960s American Orthodoxy continued to lose some of its less observant members to Conservative Judaism. At the same time, however, the Orthodox community was strengthened by a postwar influx of East European Orthodox immigrants from Europe and the coming of age of more religiously strict children of modern Orthodox families. After decades of steady erosion in levels of religious observance, the pendulum began to swing in the other direction, at least for some segments of the Orthodox community.[19]

R. Joseph continued advocating a centrist religious path, amid what he regarded as alarming signs of a religious shift to the right among some of KJ's own rank and file during the 1960s and later. In a note to his son—he would often put his suggestions to Haskel in writing—the elder Rabbi Lookstein in 1968 warned against what he called the "*chnokerization*" of KJ, that is, a tendency on the part of some members to put exaggerated focus on observances that were customary rather than required by Jewish law. He urged Haskel to remain steadfast in resisting such trends. As for those at the other end of the KJ religious spectrum, R. Joseph never compromised on KJ's official fealty to basic Orthodox principles, but he refrained from pressuring less observant congregants to become more scrupulous in their personal practice. His sermons typically commented on news events or important Jewish principles rather than admonishing his listeners over their level of observance. He was convinced that by setting the proper example and creating an attractive environment, he could "make Conservatism or Reform unnecessary and undesirable to a substantial number of families in the neighborhood."[20]

Although he was competing with Conservatism and Reform, R. Joseph approached non-Orthodox Jews with utmost respect and civility, and he taught his son to do likewise. "My father loved every Jew, no matter what his state of religiosity, piety or observance," R. Haskel noted. "He used to say, 'The only Jew I don't love is one who doesn't love other Jews.'" Significantly, his father "was prepared to meet every Jew where he was, and, through warmth and genuine affection, he tried to bring him closer to tradition. Kehilath Jeshurun and Ramaz were built on this foundation of love and acceptance."[21] It is noteworthy that in 1959 a front-page report in the *KJ Bulletin* describing recent academic achievements by "young people of K.J." announced with evident pride that one young man "was ordained as Rabbi by the Jewish Theological Seminary," Conservative Judaism's rabbinical institution. On a similar note, the speaker chosen to deliver the sermon following Thanksgiving Day services in 1962 was a professor at Reform Judaism's rabbinical seminary, Hebrew Union College, and was involved in a Bible translation project, no less—and was identified as such in the KJ newsletter.[22] This open approach to intra-Jewish relations reflected both Joseph Lookstein's personality and his philosophy of Jewish communal life. His son would do likewise. For example, when Rabbi Dr. Mordecai Kaplan, founder of Reconstructionist Judaism, passed away in 1983, R. Haskel placed a paid obituary for him in the *New York Times*, acknowledging that Kaplan had once been an assistant rabbi at KJ and praising his intellectual contributions to American Jewish life.[23] In a similar spirit, R. Haskel in 1986 invited a Conservative rabbi, Reuven Kimmelman, to serve as Scholar in Residence for KJ's Annual Synagogue Shabbaton.[24]

Compassion was another trait that R. Haskel absorbed from his forebears. According to Lookstein family lore, a woman once came to the RaMaZ on a Friday afternoon with a chicken that had a hole in its stomach. She wanted to know if it was kosher. Rabbi Margolies and R. Joseph inspected the chicken together. The younger rabbi felt certain that the chicken had swallowed a sharp object which had punctured its stomach, one of the eighteen primary criteria for deciding that something is nonkosher. The RaMaZ took a sefer from his bookshelf and located a similar case in which an early halakhic authority had permitted eating the chicken. He then found a second rabbinical authority, in another sefer, who had likewise issued a lenient ruling in such a case. "This is a poor woman," Rabbi Margolies told R. Joseph. "If we declare her chicken to be *treif* she will have nothing to eat for Shabbos. Let's rely on these two [authorities] and you take a little responsibility on your shoulders and I'll take some on my shoulders and let this woman have a good Shabbos."

This, R. Haskel later wrote, was an example of the "Torat chesed" that his father learned from the RaMaZ and passed on to him. "It demonstrated [Rabbi Margolies's] care for people.... He embodied in his personality the Talmudic principle that *koach d'heteira adif*, the power to permit, is preferable to the power to prohibit." The RaMaZ "believed that it was the responsibility of a *posek* [religious authority] to make Judaism livable for people and not difficult for them," a principle R. Haskel deemed especially important "in an era like ours, where so many Orthodox Jews seem to belong to the 'Chumra of the Month Club.'"[25]

While the new assistant rabbi was in some respects his father's son—"my father was, after all, larger than life and in many ways I idolized him"—R. Haskel also had ideas of his own that he hoped to implement at KJ.

Yes, the services were very dignified, and that was appropriate, at least to a certain extent. But they were also somewhat stuffy. Men were expected to wear a black kippa in shul; if you showed up with a knitted kippa, an usher would ask you to take it off. Nor was the atmosphere child-friendly—since there was so much emphasis on the services being orderly, people were less likely to bring their children. I understood what my father was doing. He was trying to create an Orthodox synagogue in which people would feel just as comfortable as if they were in Temple Emanuel. And his approach was absolutely right for the first half of the twentieth century. But as we entered the 1960s, people's needs were starting to change. I thought it would be possible to loosen things up a little, not in terms of the content of the services, but in the overall atmosphere of the shul.[26]

One of R. Haskel's first initiatives was the creation of a Young Marrieds Club. Beginning in the autumn of 1958, the club met monthly at members' homes to discuss current social and political issues, sometimes with multiple speakers to explore issues from various angles. The inaugural meeting, for example, which focused on birth control, brought speakers to address the medical, legal, and socioeconomic aspects of the issue, with Rabbi Lookstein presenting "the Jewish view." The level of audience participation was "spotty at best," perhaps, according to R. Haskel's notes, "due to the delicate nature of the subject."[27] The next session, however, dealt with "The Parent-Child Relationship," and "everyone participated and aired his views on the subject... if success is measured by liveliness, it was quite successful," the rabbi noted.[28] The Young Marrieds Club continued to court controversy over the years. For example, one 1966 meeting focusing on the adoption of racially mixed Jewish babies generated "a heated discussion" that turned "explosive," according to the KJ newsletter.[29]

In 1958 Yeshiva University launched a Department of Adult Education to help modern Orthodox synagogues undertake their own adult learning programs. Under R. Haskel's direction, the KJ Adult Institute grew in its first two years from three courses and 25 part-time students to seven courses with 116 full-time students. Featuring classes in Talmud, Hebrew language, Jewish history, festival laws, and liturgy, the program was so popular that many of the classes in the first year were extended through the summer months. By the second year, R. Haskel reported to the Y.U. Department of Adult Education "a phenomenal rise" in the congregation's interest and participation in the program. The Jewish history class was particularly popular, with 90 registrants. Attendees in the various courses "ranged from the president of the congregation to the most recently elected member."[30] Course offerings expanded significantly in the years that followed. Hebrew calligraphy, Jewish music, and Holocaust literature joined the list, as well as a course on the New York Jewish community, taught by Malcolm Hoenlein, then executive director of the Jewish Community Relations Council, and a session on the thought of Martin Buber, taught by Professor Michael Wyschogrod.

To judge by the topics selected for various synagogue programs in the early 1960s, KJ under the Rabbis Lookstein was a congregation that was somewhat ahead of its time. For example, although the Soviet Jewry protest movement in the United States did not become a significant part of the major Jewish organizations' agenda until 1970–1971, the KJ Men's Club as early as 1964 featured a film about the plight of Soviet Jewry. Likewise, although public discussion of the world's response to the Holocaust began in earnest only with the publication of Arthur Morse's 1968 book, *While Six Million Died,* KJ's Cultural Luncheons series in 1964 and again in 1965 featured mock trials of the international community for standing idly by during the Holocaust.[31] The KJ adult education offerings were also notable for their recognition of the growing interest among women in advanced Jewish studies. A Talmud *shiur* by the noted scholar Rabbi Hershel Schachter was open to women, and although only a small number of the attendees were women, they described it as a groundbreaking experience.[32]

Some of the programs R. Haskel initiated responded to specific problems in the congregation. For example, a proposal for a "Sabbath Seudah Seminar" that he drew up in the early 1960s sought to combat indications of religious laxity during the final hours of the Sabbath day. "As the day draws slowly to a close, the tendency to ignore [the restrictions of] Shabbat becomes more pronounced," he wrote. "The violations of Shabbat afternoon can vary from a television program to an early start for an evening appointment.... Now, we regularly have an attendance of 60 to 70 men, women, and children [at Shabbat mincha services]—no mean feat in a community such as ours. I don't know what the men and women do at home when they don't come to mincha on Shabbat. The chances are that they are not saying *Gott fun Avrohom*[33] with their children as they watch the evening shadows lengthen. When they are in shul, however, I can be certain that their Shabbat is ending on the right note."

As he envisioned it, the program would consist of the mincha prayer service, a communal meal with singing, and then a discussion period that would include questions for the rabbi and a ten-minute talk by a layman [which, he felt, would increase attendance because "laymen bring their own rooting section"]. The topics to be discussed should be cleared with the rabbi first, "otherwise Jacob will be described as a cheat, Joseph a spoiled brat, and Miriam a gossiping virago, with the rabbi left to defend them." Speakers too needed to be chosen "with the utmost caution" since, as he put it, "not every layman is a Demosthenes although there will be no shortage of men and women who think they are." Not coincidentally, the *KJ Bulletin*'s report on the success of the opening program [70 people attended] asserted that speakers Fred and Rosemiriam Zuckerman spoke "with the eloquence, lucidity, and cogency of a Demosthenes." The program was so successful that R. Haskel was invited to deliver a report on it at the following year's annual convention of the Yeshiva University Rabbinic Alumni.[34]

R. Haskel invested considerable energy in developing an array of youth groups, and as early as 1961 his father noted approvingly that the KJ building was "humming with youth activity," so much so that "two doormen had to be engaged to provide adequate protection until late in the evening." A Junior Congregation program on Shabbat mornings, under the leadership of future Ramaz administrator Noam Shudofsky, grew quickly in the early 1960s, as did a group for KJ teenagers called Shachar. "Our teenage group is the only one of its kind throughout the city that does not depend upon such activities as 'Jewish basketball' and 'Jewish bowling' for its main attractions," R. Haskel proudly reported to the board of trustees in 1964. "Our young people are deeply involved in other forms of creative expression." The Father and Son Minyan, a Sunday morning program combining prayer, breakfast, and basketball, more than doubled its attendance during the 1960s, from an average of 25 in its early days to more than 50 each week. Even a storm that left 17½ inches of snow could not keep 38 men and boys from attending one Sunday in the winter of 1968.[35]

At R. Haskel's initiative, KJ also introduced a Men's Club Shabbat and a Young Couples Club Shabbat, in which congregants active in those clubs led the services in place of the regular *chazan*. "Of course not everyone was as talented as the regular *chazan*, but it was much more participatory," he noted. Later an annual "Sabbath of Welcome for New Members" was launched, with as many as 70 new members joining the Looksteins for a buffet lunch in their apartment on Shabbat.[36]

The cumulative impact of all these programs could be seen in the KJ membership's changing demographic profile. One Shabbat morning in 1965, R. Joseph—prodded, he said, by a worshipper who "remarked about the bountiful representation of young people at the services"—decided to "take the liberty of making an educated estimate" and concluded that of the 300-plus congregants on hand, "better than one third of the worshippers were between the ages of 13 and 35." This "delightful trend," he wrote, extended to other aspects of congregational life: almost 50 children attended that day's Junior Congregation; the Young Marrieds Group "now numbers some 40 couples"; KJ's teen group, Shachar, "now numbers 68 members"; and on Shabbat afternoons "the synagogue house is filled with young children who are engaged in club activities." Not too long before, he noted, the number of worshippers and club attendees "was much smaller." A 93-year-old synagogue with such an "active, young constituency" is "a happy combination of tradition and progress. ... We have every reason to hope that our greatest accomplishments are yet to come."[37]

These trends continued in the years that followed. At the 1971 annual meeting, KJ president Harry Baumgarten spoke of "a steady infusion of young and fresh blood into the veins and arteries of this old congregation." Noting that it was "a time when we hear much about young people abandoning their ancestral faith," and when "we hear sighs and groans about the rebellion of youth and about the 'new breed' which is drifting from us," he pointed with pride to the fact that "we at Kehilath Jeshurun can report that our young people are following in the footsteps of their forebears."[38]

Although R. Haskel's innovations arguably played a significant role in these advances, his father often responded cautiously to proposed changes. "This is not Kehilath Jeshurun" was the reaction R. Haskel sometimes received at first, but eventually, after further discussion and his son's prodding, the elder Rabbi Lookstein would reluctantly authorize his son to "go ahead and try it," often conceding afterwards that the change was worthwhile.

Sukkot 1971 provided a vivid example of this process. That year the first days of the holiday fell on a Monday and Tuesday. Catered meals were offered in the synagogue's Sukkah for $19 per meal, a substantial sum for those times. Ninety-two people attended the first meal, but only 45 came to lunch the next day. No meal was offered Monday night because, as R. Joseph put it, "Who wants to eat two big meals in one day?" By Tuesday lunch, attendance was down to 19. R. Haskel, who was focused on the importance of finding ways to bring the congregants together, was convinced that an important opportunity for communal celebration and bonding had been missed.

Sitting at the Tuesday lunch with his father and KJ president Harry Baumgarten, R. Haskel reported that Lincoln Square Synagogue had served TV dinners for $5 per person—and attracted 200 participants. He proposed doing likewise for Shabbat chol hamoed and, in fact, had already discussed it with a caterer. R. Joseph was indignant at the suggestion: "Absolutely not. That's not the Kehilath Jeshurun style; we will attract every freeloader around." R. Haskel was insistent, but when he saw that he was not persuading his father, he said bluntly, "If you won't try it out, my family and I will go to a private Sukkah on Friday night and Shabbat lunch. I can't sit here with a group which is so small because we have made the meals too expensive for ordinary people to afford." Baumgarten weighed in on R. Haskel's side, urging Rabbi Lookstein to give the idea a chance. The rabbi reluctantly gave in, although he was still convinced that the experience would be terrible. In actuality, 200 people attended the Friday night dinner and also returned for lunch the next day. KJ teenagers served the meals. "It was a tremendous, delightful community event," R. Haskel later recalled. "The teenagers from the shul served the meals and did a wonderful job. There was a spirit of togetherness, lots of *ruach*. My father agreed it had gone very well, but said we shouldn't do it again. I said, on the contrary, we have to do it, because that's the way to have Sukkot."

The following year the first days of Sukkot were due to fall on Shabbat and Sunday. Three months before the holiday, R. Haskel was invited to participate in a mission to the Soviet Union [see below]. He asked his father to make the necessary arrangements for another TV dinner-Sukkot event. Agreeing only with the greatest reluctance, R. Joseph became increasingly anxious about the plan as his son's date of departure approached. The elder Rabbi Lookstein predicted that the experience would be "a disaster" and expressed regret that he had ever agreed to it. R. Haskel was incommunicado for nearly the entire two weeks of his trip behind the Iron Curtain. Stopping briefly in London on his way back to the United States, he found two letters from his father waiting for him at the hotel.

> The first was postmarked the Friday before Sukkot. Sparks were flying off the page. "Hack, everything I feared is going to happen. All the cheapskates are making reservations, it's going to be a real mess. This is not KJ style. We will never do this again!" The second letter was postmarked the Monday of chol ha-moed. "Dear Hack, I have to apologize to you. I was wrong. It was fabulous. Mike Barany, the caterer, did a great job, the kids served nicely, the spirit was wonderful, the Sukkah was filled with singing. It was very very special." I give my father alot of credit for saying that. Doing it that way was not at all his style.[39]

Joseph Lookstein had built Kehilath Jeshurun according to a strategy that placed utmost emphasis on dignity and propriety. "That Sukkot, by contrast, was positively *heimish*," R. Haskel said. "It was orderly, but with a good deal of planned disorder. Teenagers instead of waiters? Paper plates and paper tablecloths instead of dishes and nice linen tablecloths? It was unheard of at KJ." R. Joseph and others of his generation were accustomed to synagogue's events that reflected the station in life that most of the congregants had attained. By contrast,

R. Haskel's approach sacrificed luxury for affordability in order to include members who were less well off.

The experience was indicative of a young assistant rabbi beginning to "loosen things up a bit," leaving his mark in ways that would ultimately facilitate the growth of the synagogue and the community around it. By 2007 KJ was serving as many as 600 people in three separate sukkahs, possibly the largest communal Sukkot celebrations in the United States at the time. The TV dinners are a thing of the past, and waiters have replaced the teenagers, but the synagogue still keeps the price low, often taking a loss in order to make the event accessible to congregants and their families of all economic levels, and even permitting participants to bring their own meals if they cannot afford the price.

In the same spirit of fostering what he called "a family feeling," R. Haskel sought to introduce the practice of singing briefly after a *misheberach* is recited at the Torah reading in celebration of a family simcha. After a *misheberach* for the birth of a girl, the song would be *Siman Tov U'Mazel Tov*; for the birth of a boy, *Ureh Vanim*; for an engagement, *Od Yishama*; for an *aufruf* [pre-wedding celebration], *Vayehi Biy'shurun Melech*. R. Haskel was not the first modern Orthodox rabbi to do this, but it represented such a sharp break from R. Joseph's regimented style that the elder rabbi Lookstein insisted his son bring the issue before the board of trustees. One trustee did, in fact, object, charging that such singing was "not in keeping with the dignity of our congregation" and warning that the assistant rabbi was "trying to turn this place into a Young Israel" by permitting a level of disorder comparable to that for which some Young Israel synagogues are known. But with R. Joseph's support, the proposal gained approval by consensus and became standard KJ practice, occasionally even branching out into a chorus of "Happy Birthday."[40]

R. Haskel's modest innovations at KJ and the father–son disagreements they occasionally engendered were all part of the apprenticeship experience. "Everything I do as a rabbi, I learned from my father," he said. "From watching him, I learned everything from preaching to running a funeral or a wedding to administration of the synagogue. He taught Practical Rabbinics and Homiletics at RIETS—but I was blessed to have the living role model." R. Joseph was also a helpful critic. "On a Shabbat when I gave the sermon, we went to his office after the services to take off our *taleism*, and he would invariably say, 'Hack, that was a very fine sermon, thoughtful and very well organized; of course, I would have said....' Sometimes, deep down, I might have bristled a bit because of the critique, but after his passing I came to miss that criticism very much. I miss having someone who will tell me straight when I am off base—the congregants are too respectful and my wife loves me too much. For a while, my daughter Debbie filled the role—walking home from shul, she would say, 'Daddy, I think that was a pretty good sermon; I would give it an A-minus,' and then she would explain why it wasn't an A."[41]

The transition from R. Joseph's leadership to R. Haskel's would have proceeded very gradually had health issues not intervened. In 1965 R. Joseph's doctor, alarmed by the rabbi's developing heart condition, ordered him to withdraw from at least one of his major areas of work. Until that time, he had served simultaneously as rabbi of KJ, principal of Ramaz, and, since 1954, acting president and then chancellor of Bar Ilan University. He chose to give up his role at Ramaz. R. Haskel replaced him.

## NOTES

[1] Ibid.

[2] Ibid.

[3] Rabbi Joseph H. Lookstein, "Rabbi Haskel Lookstein: An Evaluation and a Tribute," undated [1978], File: Rabbi Joseph Lookstein, KJ, p.3; RHL interview, 25 July 2007.

[4] RHL interview, 10 July 2007.

[5] "Haskel Lookstein Elected Assistant to Rabbi Lookstein," KJB XXV:36 [6 June 1958], p.1; "Rabbi Haskel Lookstein Installed as Assistant Rabbi in Congregation," KJB XXV:38 [20 June 1958], p.1.

[6] RHL interview, 25 July 2007.

[7] Rabbi Lookstein recounted this anecdote in a memorial article he wrote in the Spring 2003 issue of *Jewish Action*, after the Rav's passing. In that version, however,

Rabbi Lookstein did not reveal that in fact he was the student who spotted the discrepancy.

[8] Memoranda of Rabbi Haskel Lookstein's conversations with Rabbi Soloveitchik, 24 March 1982 and 1 November 1984, File: Rabbi Joseph Soloveitchik, Kehilath Jeshurun Archives, New York [hereafter KJ].

[9] Adam S. Ferziger, "The Lookstein Legacy: An American Orthodox Rabbinical Dynasty?" Jewish History12:1 [Spring 1999], pp. 128–129; Jeffrey S. Gurock, *American Jewish Orthodoxy in Historical Perspective* [Hoboken, N.J.: Ktav, 1996, p.120.

[10] Jenna Weissman Joselit, "Of Manners, Morals, and Orthodox Judaism: Decorum Within the Orthodox Synagogue," in Jeffrey S. Gurock, ed., *Ramaz: School, Community, Scholarship & Orthodoxy* [Hoboken, N.J.: Ktav, 1989], p.24.

[11] Joselit, op.cit., p. 27.

[12] Ferziger, "Lookstein Legacy," p.131

[13] Joselit, op.cit., pp. 40, 65.

[14] Joseph H. Lookstein, "The Handshake," KJB XLIV:4 [12 November 1976], p.3.

[15] "Appropriate Attire for the House of God," KJB XXXIV:3 [17 September 1965], p.1.

[16] "Hakafoth at Kehilath Jeshurun," KJB XXXIV:5 [8 October 1965], p. 3.

[17] "Ramaz and Shachar Weekend Attracts Exuberant Gathering of Teenagers," KJB XXXIII:34 [28 May 1965], p.1.

[18] Jeffrey S. Gurock, "The Winnowing of American Orthodoxy," *Approaches to Modern Judaism* II [1984], pp. 41–54.

[19] Jeffrey S. Gurock, "From Fluidity to Rigidity: The Religious Worlds of Conservative and Orthodox Jews in Twentieth Century America," David W. Belin Lecture in American Jewish Affairs [Ann Arbor: University of Michigan, 1998], p.14.

[20] Ferziger, "Lookstein Legacy," pp. 130–131.

[21] Rabbi Haskel Lookstein, "Words of Eulogy," undated [1979], File: Rabbi Joseph Lookstein, KJ, p.5.

[22] "Young People of K.J. Advance Academically," KJB XVII:37 [19 June 1959], p. 1; "Dr. Harry M. Orlinsky to Discuss New Bible Translation at Thanksgiving Service," KJB XXXI:9 [16 November 1962], p. 1.

[23] R. Haskel credits his mother, Gertrude Lookstein, for the suggestion to place the obituary.

[24] "Rabbi Reuven Kimmelman to Be Scholar in Residence at Annual Synagogue Shabbaton," KJB LIII:6 [21 March 1986], p. 3; "Face to Face with Pope John Paul," KJB LV:2 [12 October 1987], p. 3.

25 "The Ramaz on His 70th Yahrzeit—A Sermon of Tribute by His Great Grandson, Rabbi Haskel Lookstein, Shabbat Ki Tetze," September 2, 2006, File: Rabbi Moses Margolies, KJ, pp. 3–4.

26 RHL interview, 10 July 2007.

27 "Young Marrieds Meeting No. 2, November 15, 1958," File: Young Marrieds, KJ.

28 "Young Marrieds Meeting No. 3, January 10, 1959," File: Young Marrieds, KJ.

29 "Rabbi Isaac N. Trainin Addresses Young Marrieds on Matter of Great Concern," KJB XXXIV:30 [29 April 1966].

30 Martin Markson, "Adult Institute" [undated], File: Adult Institute, KJ.

31 "Another Capacity Audience Attends Men's Club Meeting," Kehilath Jeshurun Bulletin XXXIII:11 [21 November 1964], 1; "Report on Activities of Congregation Kehilath Jeshurun 1964–1965" [New York: Kehilath Jeshurun, 1965], pp. 8, 21; "Cultural Luncheon Serves as Forum for Youth," Kehilath Jeshurun Bulletin XXXII:27 [27 March 1964], p. 4.

32 Kritz interview.

33 A Yiddish-language prayer recited by some Orthodox Jews shortly before the conclusion of Shabbat.

34 Rabbi Haskel Lookstein "A Sabbath Afternoon Program" [undated], File: Sabbath Seudah Seminar, KJ; "Sabbath Seudah Seminar Opens Auspiciously," KJB XXVI:9 [7 November 1958], p. 3; "Rabbi Haskel Lookstein Reads Paper Before Rabbinic Alumni," KJB XXVIII:10[13 November 1959], p. 2.

35 Rabbi Joseph Lookstein, "Father and Son Minyan Report," undated [apparently 1968], File: Father–Son Minyan, KJ; Minutes of the KJ Board of Trustees, 3 December 1961, p. 6; RHL, "Youth Activities Report, November 8, 1964," in Minutes of the KJ Board of Trustees, 8 November 1964, p. 2.

36 RHL; "Special Projects Committee—Minutes of First Meeting held in two parts on May 23 and 29, 1974,"File: Special; Projects, KJ, p. 7; Audrey Lookstein interview with Rafael Medoff, 20 January 2008.

37 "Young People in a 93 Year Old Congregation," KJB XXXIII:1 [22 January 1965], p. 3.

38 Mr. Harry W. Baumgarten, "President's Address, Annual Meeting, Congregation Kehilath Jeshurun, May 4, 1971, " p. 3.

39 RHL interview, 25 July 2007.

40 Minutes of Meeting of the Board of Trustees, March 25, 1971, pp. 8–9.

41 Mindy, Debbie, and Shira Lookstein memoir in Teacher, Preacher, p. 94; Debbie Senders interview with Rafael Medoff, 5 February 2008.

# III. HUSBAND AND FATHER

While devoting himself to building the "KJ family," R. Haskel was also building a family of his own. In late 1958 he began dating Audrey Katz, a teacher at the Ramaz elementary school whom he had first met when they were both active in Mizrachi Hatzair, the youth wing of the Mizrachi religious Zionist movement. She was impressed from the start by his warmth, considerate nature, and strongly positive outlook on life. After a six-month courtship, Haskel and Audrey were married in the spring of 1959. Their first child, Mindy, was born in 1961. Debbie followed two years later, then Shira in 1966 and Joshua in 1970. As assistant rabbi at KJ and assistant principal and instructor at Ramaz, R. Haskel juggled an array of professional responsibilities. The bulk of the child rearing naturally fell to Audrey—"which is why they turned out so well," he later quipped—although he tried to be home for dinner each evening and in general to play as active a role in their family life as his hectic schedule permitted.

To R. Haskel, Audrey was always his "anchor," the one who "keeps me balanced" and who always exhibited "an uncanny ability to instinctively know what's right, what to do in particular situations." Her caring nature, her generous approach to tzedakah both in terms of their financial contributions and the time she devoted to volunteering, and her selflessness—"of which I am the prime beneficiary," as he put it—are what he credited for making it possible for him to accomplish everything he has done in the world outside their home.[1]

The Lookstein children still have vivid and pleasant memories of how their father incorporated their needs into his crowded daily routine. When R. Haskel needed to inspect the kashrut of the Burry Best cookie factory each month, it became a fun outing [for whichever of the children could wake up at 4:30 A.M.]. The teens were able to get driving lessons on the narrow roads of a cemetery after an unveiling concluded. Entertainment sometimes meant opera tickets that someone had given to the rabbi, "with special pre-opera appreciation lessons on the living room couch thrown in for good measure," as they put it. "So while we didn't always get the gifts that other kids got, we got the greatest gift of all—Daddy."[2]

Family vacation time offered a more substantial break from the daily routine. From 1963 until 1970, summers were spent in a rented house at Lake Mohegan. In a reverse of the typical New York Orthodox family's summer vacation routine, R. Haskel stayed with Audrey and the children during the week but returned to KJ for each Shabbat. In 1971, when Mindy and Debbie were old enough to attend Camp Massad, the rest of the family began going there too. R. Haskel assumed the position of camp rabbi and tennis instructor. Some children would regard the presence of their parents in their summer camp as an unnerving intrusion on their private space. The Lookstein children, however, recall feeling no such unease; in fact, Shira enjoyed seeing them there, feeling that her personal identity was intertwined with them and strengthened by their presence.[3]

There were vacations in the winter as well. These often consisted of a 23-hour drive, straight through the night, to south Florida. They would stay for a week or so with the elder Looksteins, who by then had taken to spending that time of year in the warmer climate. Even on vacation, R. Haskel felt a strong sense of responsibility to the KJ community, a perception of himself as a "servant of the people" who must "always be there" for their needs. This meant interrupting his vacation time to answer phone calls from congregants, help them resolve pressing problems, and console them in times of grief. Sometimes it meant cutting the family's vacation short and leaving Florida—or even Israel— earlier than planned so he could visit someone who had fallen gravely ill or could deliver the eulogy at a funeral. In one instance he was already at Kennedy Airport with his mother-in-law, wife, and three of their children, preparing to leave for Israel, when he received a call informing him that the wife of a former chair of the Ramaz board had suddenly become extremely ill. R. Haskel rushed to the hospital to visit her; two days later he officiated at her funeral. He then joined the family in Israel.

Through it all, the Looksteins strove to maintain as normal a home life as possible. Shabbat was still Shabbat, with its special atmosphere, homemade delicacies, and parents prodding children to join in singing *zmirot* (Shira's lack of cooperation earned her the nickname "Lo Shira," ['doesn't sing,' in Hebrew]). More than one prominent visiting rabbi found his shoelaces tied together by young mischief-makers. Almost every Shabbat table in the Lookstein home included guests, whether KJ members, cousins, or celebrities, some of whom became close personal friends, such as the families of Israeli diplomats Chaim Herzog and Yehuda Blum. The Lookstein children, weary of listening to their father share all-too-familiar anecdotes with the Shabbat guests, later fondly recalled their delight at discovering that the children of the famous violinist Yitzhak Perlman were likewise bored to the point of snickering and eye-rolling when their father shared timeworn anecdotes with R. Haskel and Audrey. The abundance of Shabbat guests left its mark; all four Lookstein children regard the plethora of guests at their own tables as the product of their childhood experiences. Especially true to form, a prominent Israeli diplomat in Atlanta is today a frequent guest at Mindy's Shabbat table.[4]

Daily life in the Lookstein home featured the same array of joys and conflicts that one finds anywhere, irrespective of R. Haskel's role in the school and synagogue. Report cards were still a source of tension between parents and children. Birthdays were still celebrated with parties or outings to Shea Stadium. Teenagers were still admonished to cut short their long-distance phone calls, unless they happened to be speaking with their married siblings. And children, even as adults, still turned to their parents for advice. Josh, as a young rabbi in his first pulpit [in Stamford, Connecticut], sometimes telephoned his father a dozen or more times in a single day for guidance on various synagogue issues. "He took my calls every single time—he never even said he would call me back in a few minutes, he spoke to me right then, whenever I needed him." From his family's point of view, that willingness to make himself available to anyone in need is one of R. Haskel's most admirable qualities. "He does not know the concept of turning down a request," according to Josh. "His sense of responsibility is really extraordinary." Although Josh later became a professional in the world of Jewish philanthropy rather than a pulpit rabbi, he continued to call on his father for guidance and found him always available.

Josh noted that from his earliest days in the rabbinate, R. Haskel chose to attend an inordinate number of his congregants' life cycle events, whether bar mitzvahs, consoling mourners, engagement parties, hospital visits, bar and bat mitzvahs, or weddings. "He attends probably more than three hundred such events each year," Josh estimated. "And when he and my mother go to a wedding, they don't necessarily leave after the *chuppah*, as most rabbis would do. They frequently stay all the way until the very end of the evening."[5]

"Haskel's attitude in such situations is that while a particular simcha might be the second or third such event for us that weekend, it's the only simcha for that particular family," Audrey noted. "He tries hard to put himself in the other person's shoes so that he can be sensitive to their needs and concerns." This level of dedication requires an extraordinary amount of energy on R. Haskel's part, which KJ members find both admirable and remarkable. They note that when he leads a public Passover seder, as for example during a mission to Israel, R. Haskel is on his feet virtually the entire time, nearly four hours of speaking, reading, and going from table to table to encourage everyone's participation and discussion. Similarly, on Yom Kippur, between the portions of the service he leads in KJ's auxiliary minyan and those he leads in the main minyan, he is standing nearly the entire time.[6]

In addition to celebrations of congregants and Ramaz alumni, the Looksteins' calendar has always been crowded with simchas of cousins, nephews, and nieces.

R. Haskel maintained a close relationship with his sister Nathalie [d. 2004], her four children, and sixteen grandchildren. "Haskel was always very devoted to his nephews and nieces, and even more so since Nathalie's passing," Audrey pointed out. The families are scrupulous about participating in each other's simchas, to the point of refraining from choosing dates for the events until everyone's availability is confirmed.[7]

**NOTES**

[1] RHL Interview, 12 February 2008.

[2] Shira Baruch interview with Rafael Medoff, 15 January 2008; Debbie Senders interview.

[3] Debbie Senders interview; Shira Baruch interview; Audrey Lookstein interview; Mindy Cinnamon interview with Rafael Medoff, 17 January 2008; Joshua Lookstein interview with Rafael Medoff, 11 January 2008.

[4] Ibid.

[5] Joshua Lookstein interview.

[6] Audrey Lookstein interview; Debbie Senders interview.

[7] Audrey Lookstein interview.

# IV. THE SCHOLAR

R. Haskel's additional responsibilities at Ramaz compelled him to cut back in the area of his own education. As a rabbinical student at RIETS, he was required to simultaneously complete a master's degree at Y.U.'s Bernard Revel Graduate School. In 1963 he earned an M.A. in Medieval Jewish History and Philosophy, with a master's thesis on "The Organization of Maimonides' Sefer Ha-Mitzvot," under the supervision of Professor Irving Agus. He described Agus as "a major intellectual influence on my life."

In the years that followed, R. Haskel inched his way toward a Ph.D. in Jewish History, gradually completing the requisite coursework as time allowed, particularly during the summer. In late 1972 he presented his doctoral advisory committee with a proposed topic for his dissertation: a follow-up study of Ramaz alumni. The committee rejected the topic on the grounds that it was more sociology than history. Committee members also wondered whether the principal of Ramaz could be truly objective in studying his own former students. At a social occasion a few days after the committee's decision, Jerry Goodman, executive director of the National Conference on Soviet Jewry, suggested to the visibly downcast rabbi that he consider writing a dissertation comparing American Jewry's response to the persecution of Soviet Jews to its response to news of the Holocaust. "Bells went off in my head," he remembered. "I was incredibly excited. It was as if I had just been reborn as a doctoral student." R. Haskel had long exhibited a particular interest in the Holocaust. As early as 1963 the topic he had chosen for his remarks at a Youth Sabbath at KJ was "the relationship of the Warsaw Ghetto to the current crisis in Israel," as the *KJ Bulletin* put it. Now here was an opportunity to study a topic that combined his interest in the Holocaust and his own continuing experiences in the Soviet Jewry struggle.[1]

Two colleagues helped refine the topic. Professor Hyman Grinstein urged him to focus on the Holocaust period alone, since the Soviet Jewry movement was too new to study as history. Elie Wiesel—a friend and, at the time, a member of KJ—suggested that instead of trying to cover the entire vast period of the Holocaust, he should take five or six specific episodes or narrow periods. In the spring of 1973 R. Haskel set to work on "The Public Response of American Jews to the Holocaust, 1938–1944." The months stretched into years as the dissertation research vied for his attention with his heavy load of work at the school and the synagogue.

Three factors ultimately provided the final push to complete the dissertation. The first was Audrey's insistence that instead of his teaching at Camp Massad in the summer, as he had been doing for years, they should stay home for one or more summers until he finished the work. He ended up spending the summers of 1976, 1977, and 1978 in New York City. The second factor was the position of Revel dean Dr. Haym Soloveitchik. In the autumn of 1977 the dean gave R. Haskel a deadline of December 1978 to complete the dissertation or face termination of his student status and loss of all his credits. The ultimatum compelled R. Haskel to drop a number of projects that were draining his time but were not necessary to his basic responsibilities at Ramaz and KJ. The third factor was the influence of his father. "He said to me, 'Hack, you have to finish your dissertation and you have to do it now—otherwise, something will happen to get in the way and then you'll never get it done.'" R. Joseph spoke from experience: after completing his own M.A. in sociology at City College, he had been studying for a doctorate and even had selected a topic for his dissertation, but the outbreak of World War II and its consequences made it impossible for him to complete it. He feared something similar would happen to his son.

Two prominent scholars of American Jewish history, one a veteran and the other a newcomer, participated in overseeing the dissertation process. Professor Henry Feingold of CUNY initially served as his advisor for the dissertation, and Professor Jeffrey Gurock, who, ironically, had once been a student in R. Haskel's American Jewish history class at Ramaz, was assigned to refine his writing style, "essentially to remove all traces of homiletics from his history."[2] The dissertation was finalized in March 1979, and father and son proudly strode together in cap and gown at the Yeshiva University graduation ceremony in May. "I remember my father's absolute delight at seeing me complete what he had never been privileged to finish in his career," R. Haskel recalled. "But my father also proved prescient. Two months after the Y.U. graduation he died from a stroke. My life changed radically. Had I not finished the dissertation then, it would never have been completed. Something had happened, as he predicted."[3]

The impetus to publish the dissertation as a book came from R. Haskel's uncle, Bernard Fishman. He felt strongly that it was important for American Jewry to face up to its record during the Holocaust, and that it would be helpful to his nephew's standing in the community for his scholarly achievement to be brought to public attention. Fishman, an attorney and activist with a wide range of contacts, shared copies of the dissertation with associates in the publishing world and found considerable interest.[4]

Published as *Were We Our Brothers' Keepers? The Public Response of American Jews to the Holocaust, 1938–1944*, the dissertation was released in hardcover by Hartmore House in 1985 and then in paperback in 1988 by Random House, with a foreword by Elie Wiesel. "Unbelievable but true: the American Jewish community had not responded to the heart-rending cries of their brothers and sisters in Nazified Europe," Wiesel wrote. "At the very least, not as they should have.... Too harsh a judgment? Rabbi Haskel Lookstein judges no one.

No one has the right to judge. Lookstein can only relate his own pain. It overwhelms us. It reflects a broken heart. But a broken heart is an open heart, open to suffering and to prayer, to anger and to hope, to hope in spite of anger, to faith too, to faith in spite of despair."[5]

Focusing on major events of the Holocaust period such as Kristallnacht, the confirmation of the Nazi genocide, and the Allies' refugee conference at Bermuda, R. Haskel analyzed the Jewish community's response in each instance, as reflected through Jewish and general periodicals. The result was an incisive yet readable portrait of a community anxious to help its persecuted brethren but handicapped by intraorganizational rivalries, fears of stirring domestic anti-Semitism if they protested too loudly, and most of all, a business-as-usual mentality among Jewish leaders, who failed to recognize the urgency of the crisis.

*Were We Our Brothers' Keepers?* broke important new ground. Although several major scholarly studies of the American government's response to the Holocaust were published in the late 1970s and early 1980s, and those books had included some material on American Jews, Lookstein's was the first book-length scholarly study of the American Jewish community's response to the Holocaust. His final paragraph summed up both the book's findings and his personal philosophy: "The Final Solution may have been unstoppable by American Jewry, but it should have been unbearable for them. And it wasn't. This is important, not alone for our understanding of the past, but for our sense of responsibility in the future."[6]

The book nearly sold out its hardcover print run of 5,000, and the paperback did almost as well. The reviews were overwhelmingly positive. Professor Deborah Lipstadt praised it as "most important," and the worst that Professor Edward Shapiro, a critic, could charge was that R. Haskel had indulged in "moralism," but an undue emphasis on morality is not an accusation at which the rabbi necessarily took offense. Not surprisingly, readers took from the book a variety of lessons, depending on their particular perspective. U.S. Senator Howard Metzenbaum [D-OH], for example, wondered, "Are we going through some of the same in our indifference to the effort to Christianize America now?" A letter writer in a Florida Jewish newspaper charged that "too many Jewish leaders spend their time fighting for other people's causes—a sad fact which suggests that they really have not learned the lessons from the silence of the Jewish leadership during the Holocaust."[7]

Significantly, a number of prominent figures in the Jewish establishment responded sympathetically to the book despite R. Haskel's criticism of the 1940s Jewish leadership. "Through Haskel Lookstein's volume, we must finally acknowledge our error," wrote Philadelphia Jewish leader Rabbi David Wortman. "We must commit ourselves to never again be silent in the face of the banality of evil and the stark reality of human suffering." Council of Jewish Federations vice president Donald Feldstein commended "Lookstein's honest examination ... he writes in sorrow and not in anger, and has therefore produced a useful, true, and valuable document."[8]

The positive reception that greeted *Were We Our Brothers' Keepers?* may be attributed to a number of factors. First, the research was solid and the tone of the writing was measured. It was scholarship, not a polemic. Second, the author was a widely respected figure in the Jewish community, someone with a track record of credibility and integrity. Third, American Jewry had matured sufficiently to be able to take a sober look at the controversies of the 1940s. It might not have been possible for such a book to have gained a serious audience in the 1960s or early 1970s. The memories of the Holocaust and the intra-Jewish quarrels of that period were still too fresh. The publication of the first books critiquing the Roosevelt administration's response to the Holocaust, Arthur Morse's *While Six Million Died* and David Wyman's *Paper Walls*, both published in 1968, made it easier for American Jews to begin looking at their own record. The rise and fall of the Goldberg Commission, a group of Jewish leaders and scholars who during 1981–1983 examined the U.S. Jewish response to the Holocaust, stirred controversy but also helped pave the way for the community to consider the subject. Most of all, the passage of time since the Holocaust brought to the fore a new generation of American Jews for whom the partisan battles of the 1940s were irrelevant. *Were We Our Brothers' Keepers?* asked the right questions at a time when American Jews were finally ready to ask them too.

R. Haskel's research findings assumed a central role in his view of the American Jewish community, past and present. The Jewish leadership's response to news of the Holocaust became the quintessential model of how Jewish leaders should not behave. In his speeches, writings, and classes in the years that followed, he would often cite the failures of the 1940s in commenting on issues such as the plight of Soviet Jewry, the threats facing Israel, and the consequences of Jewish disunity.

One episode in particular vividly illustrated Rabbi Lookstein's application of the lessons of the Holocaust period to contemporary situations. Shortly before Purim in 1996 a wave of Arab terrorist attacks left 63 Israelis dead and more than 200 wounded. R. Haskel, who in his book had bemoaned the failure of American Jews in the 1940s to alter their daily behavior patterns in response to the news of the Nazi killings, decided to drastically alter KJ's Purim services and celebration. Upon entering the synagogue that evening for the reading of the megillah, worshippers found the ark draped with a black curtain, and some of the lights in the sanctuary extinguished. In his explanatory remarks, R. Haskel said that in view of the murders in Israel, "it would be impossible for us to conduct business as usual in our observance of Purim.... The fact that it happened six thousand miles away was irrelevant. In our minds, it happened in our own neighborhood." Thus, before the *Megillat Esther* reading, special prayers were recited for the terror victims; KJ's post-megillah pizza party and Vice Presidents' Breakfast, and Ramaz's annual Purim Chagiga, were canceled; and the singing, dancing, and Purim Spiel which were the most prominent feature of KJ's communal Purim Seuda were eliminated. Just before the holiday began, Rabbis Lookstein and Bakst addressed the student body of Ramaz on the importance of recognizing that "our family suffered a loss and, while Purim had to be observed in a proper halakhic manner, there was no room for joy and festivity."[9]

# NOTES

[1] KJB XXXI:33 [17 May 1963], p. 2.

[2] Jeffrey S. Gurock, "Called to the Principal's Office in Triumph," in *Teacher, Preacher*, p. 26.

[3] RHL interview, 10 January 2008.

[4] Ibid.

[5] Elie Wiesel, "Foreword," in Haskel Lookstein, *Were We Our Brothers' Keepers? The Public Response of American Jews to the Holocaust, 1938–1944* [New York: Vintage Books, 1988], pp. 9, 11.

[6] Haskel Lookstein, *Were We Our Brothers' Keepers*, p. 216.

[7] Deborah E. Lipstadt, "America and the Holocaust," *Modern Judaism* 10:3 [October 1990], p. 290; Edward S. Shapiro, "Historians and the Holocaust: The Role of American Jewry," *Congress Monthly*, May /June 1986, p. 7; Howard M. Metzenbaum to RHL, 20 March 1986, File: Book, KJ; Sarah Stein, "Have Jewish Leaders Learned Their Lessons?" [letter], Miami Jewish Tribune, 2 December 1988. Surprisingly, Henry L. Feingold, who had been R. Haskel's advisor for the first few chapters of the dissertation and at that time did not dispute its main contentions, wrote in *American Historical Review* [vol. 91, pp. 1015–1016] that R. Haskel's central argument was "unsubstantiated."

[8] Rabbi David A. Wortman, "*Book Review: Were We Our Brothers' Keepers?*" *Jewish Exponent of Philadelphia*, 27 December 1985; Donald Feldstein, "Book Review*: Were We Our Brothers' Keepers?*" *Journal of Jewish Communal Service* 61:2–3 [Spring–Summer 1986], pp. 273–275.

[9] RHL, "A Memorable Purim But One We Would Not Like to Repeat," KJB LXV:3 [22 March 1996], p. 2.

# V. ON HIS OWN

Six weeks after his son's graduation, Joseph Lookstein, then living part time in Florida, suffered a major stroke. R. Haskel recalled:

My sister and I rushed to Miami to be with him. The first two days, Thursday and Friday, we couldn't get a smile out of him no matter how hard we tried. On Shabbat morning, I came back to the hospital after attending services at a shul nearby, one of the major synagogues in Miami Beach. Of course my father was very interested to hear my report. I said, "It was such a *balagan* [chaotic] in there—it was so noisy before the Torah reading that the rabbi had to wait five minutes for everyone to quiet down, and the same thing happened before he began his sermon. I looked around and it seemed like the congregation was similar to ours—a mixture of some older people and some younger, some refugees and some American-born, some wealthier and some less so. If we're not careful, KJ could become just like that."

R. Joseph broke into a big smile and said to Nathalie, "You know, twenty-one years of talking to your brother hasn't been in vain." To R. Haskel, the exchange demonstrated that despite their occasional disagreements, his father recognized that they were on the same page in their approach to Judaism and Jewish communal life. "Which, in fact, we were," he noted. "I believed in the same things that he believed in: a dignified synagogue, with proper decorum that befits a House of God; a modern, centrist approach to Judaism and everything that went with it; tolerance for people with whom we don't agree; and a love for all Jews."

On July 13, two weeks after his stroke, Rabbi Joseph Lookstein died. It was late on a Friday afternoon; R. Haskel, his sister Nathalie, and their mother returned to their parents' apartment to prepare for Shabbat. As his mother set the table, she directed Haskel to R. Joseph's seat. "You sit there—that was dad's seat," she said. "That's where you should sit now." A few minutes later she added, "Well, now you'll finally have a nice office," implying that R. Haskel would move from his much smaller office into R. Joseph's. "In those two comments," R. Haskel observed, "my mother took away a huge burden of guilt which I would have experienced. She matter-of-factly told me what my new role was and that I should assume it without guilt." In the months and years following his father's death, R. Haskel often turned to his mother for advice, whether on personal matters or on the contents of his sermons.

Groomed for more than two decades to inherit from his father the mantle of rabbinic and communal leadership, R. Haskel was professionally and temperamentally well suited for this role. He had, in fact, already been gradually filling his father's shoes as R. Joseph's day-to-day involvement in KJ and Ramaz diminished in his later years. Over the course of his 21 years as assistant rabbi, R. Haskel had assumed increasing responsibility for programming, mastered the techniques of running the KJ prayer service, and perfected the art of the sermon. He had also played a significant role in the many administrative functions that his father had assumed, including financial matters such as budget preparation and fundraising. On his tenth anniversary as assistant rabbi, R. Haskel expressed his gratitude for his "upbringing in a rabbinic household where the entire family lived rabonus....To see the example of one who lives his rabbinate day and night, who avoided any outside interest that was not germane, who was absorbed in and totally committed to his singular role of rabbi in Israel—as preacher, as teacher, as 'pastor.'..."[1]

One of the important tasks R. Haskel assumed after his father's passing was tending to the needs of individual members. This was the "Torat chesed" that his great grandfather had passed on to his father, and that his father had taught him. R. Haskel understood from early on that this was a role the modern rabbi is expected to fulfill. In an essay he wrote in 1960, shortly after becoming assistant rabbi, he compared the job description of the "old-time" rabbi with that of a contemporary rabbi, and he cited "the function of personal contact" as a major new requirement. "Visits to houses of mourning, participation in family events and 'simchas,' routine entertaining of members and friends of the congregation, and a day-to-day concern for people and their problems now serve as the real, perhaps the only, way in which the rabbi can 'make Jews' as it were," he wrote.[2]

Most KJ members seemed to agree that R. Haskel excelled in that area in particular. KJ's office files bulge with testimonials from appreciative members recalling Rabbi Lookstein going to great lengths to visit a sick person, console a mourner, or help someone in distress. A congregant who underwent a lengthy hospitalization, which caused him considerable financial strain, discovered that the rabbi had been secretly paying some of his medical bills.[3] A father on his way to his son's bar mitzvah on the Lower East Side was stranded in a hailstorm when his car broke down on the FDR Drive; Rabbi Lookstein, concerned about the man's tardiness, drove uptown to search for him and rescued him in time for the simcha.[4] A Ramaz ninth grader who attended a Passover seder at the rabbi's home recalled how after she accidentally spilled grape juice on the Looksteins' tablecloth, the rabbi insisted that everybody spill a little wine on the table so she would not be embarrassed.[5] An unnecessary autopsy and delayed burial of a congregant's parent was prevented by Rabbi Lookstein's swift intervention with city officials, on Shabbat.[6] When a baby was born to a congregant at a New York hospital that did not allow circumcisions to be performed by anyone other than its own surgeons, the hospital was compelled to permit the baby to be taken briefly from the hospital for a traditional *brit milah*, as a result of R. Haskel's behind-the-scenes lobbying efforts.[7] Tribute books presented to Rabbi Lookstein on the occasions of his twenty-fifth and fortieth years in the KJ pulpit, and on his seventieth birthday, overflow with letters citing acts of chesed large and small, a word of consolation at just the right moment, a thoughtful gesture just when it mattered most, an unexpected visit to the sick, a simcha invigorated by his enthusiastic participation.

Chesed was something that Rabbi Lookstein has not only always practiced, but taught as well. In a 1983 Rosh Hashana sermon titled "If You Were God," R. Haskel proposed that the most appropriate way to emulate God is to "imitate His kindness" by engaging in practical deeds of chesed. "I don't want money, I want time," he told the congregation. "No checks; instead, an effort." On Yom Kippur every KJ attendee received a card with twelve fold-down tabs, each tab corresponding to a particular area of chesed: hosting Shabbat guests, keeping in contact with the homebound elderly, visiting the sick, consoling mourners, arranging *shiduchim*, assisting the *chevra kaddisha* [burial society], and more—including "Adopt a Beginner: Open your home to a newcomer to Judaism." In 1987 the chesed campaign was expanded to include a Kol Nidre night food drive, in which all congregants on their way to the Yom Kippur evening service were asked to deposit cans of food for the homeless in barrels in the KJ lobby. At about the same time, the KJ Social Action Committee began organizing a group of volunteers to take part in the Dorot Food Distribution Project to assist impoverished elderly Jews in Manhattan.[8]

As senior rabbi of KJ, R. Haskel also now took on the responsibility for guarding against moral backsliding among his congregants. In his 1980 Rosh Hashana sermon, which generated a particularly enthusiastic response from congregants, Rabbi Lookstein advocated what he called "Menschliness Before Godliness." Too many "in our religiously resurgent Jewish world insist on *glatt kosher* but not necessarily *glatt yosher*—perfectly smooth lungs in an animal but not perfectly straight behavior in people," he declared, arguing that meticulousness in observance of religious rituals needed to be matched by a similar level of concern for ethics. Yeshiva students selling Regents exams, Orthodox businessmen evading taxes, and shul-goers indulging in gossip all make the same mistake of forgetting that Judaism's ethical regulations are as sacred as all the other mitzvot. "One cannot be a tzaddik without being a mensch first." He later described that sermon as "probably the most impactful address I have ever delivered" and said it was "the stimulus for many policies and activities in KJ and Ramaz" in the years that followed.[9]

Six years later R. Haskel returned to the subject, but this time from the other side: "If Menschliness Before Godliness, Then Why Godliness?" was the title of his Rosh Hashana sermon in 1986. If the main goal of Judaism is to be a mensch—"good, kind, caring, honest, respectful, and decent"—then "what difference does it make whether I put a metal cover on my stove on Shabbat or not"—that is, why is it necessary to observe the various Jewish rituals? Rabbi Lookstein pinpointed the three key philosophical arguments for pursuit of Godliness: "Without a sense of God and mitzvot, we would have no clear criteria for what is ethical and good; without a belief that menschliness is Divinely prescribed, most people would soon become lax in the fulfillment of ethical obligations such as giving charity or visiting the sick; and menschliness is the prerequisite to *kedusha* [holiness], which is the real goal of Judaism.[10]

Curbing ostentatious spending also became an important part of R. Haskel's creed. Luxuries and lavish simchas send the wrong message about priorities, he argued. The concept of *hatzne'a lechet*, walking humbly before God, means exercising moderation in all areas of life. Materialism run amok contradicts Judaism. He applauded a proclamation by Israeli rabbis declining to preside at simchas where the costs exceeded specified limits.[11] The manner in which bar and bat mitzvahs were celebrated became a matter of particular concern in the 1980s, as wealthier members of the American Orthodox community increasingly indulged in extraordinarily expensive events, sometimes including inappropriate entertainment, when their sons and daughters came of age.

A *New York Times* feature story in 1996, "Mitzvah or Mania?" cast an uncomfortable spotlight on events such as "Mollywood," an over-the-top Academy Awards-themed bat mitzvah celebration, complete with palm trees, singing waiters, and Oscar statuettes. Rabbi Lookstein's subsequent sermon on "Mollywood Madness" pleaded with his followers to recognize that bar and bat mitzvahs were too often characterized by wastefulness, unhealthy competition ["competition is not a bad thing in sports, scholarship, or business—but competition in consumption?"], and a diminution of kedusha, the spirit of holiness that should dominate a Jewish religious event.[12] "Bash Mitzvahs!" a 1998 story in *New York Magazine* about six-figure bar mitzvah extravaganzas, likewise discomfited some members of the congregation, but Rabbi Lookstein titled his March 7, 1998, sermon "Thank You, *New York Magazine*," arguing that while the article was a "caricature," it also contained "an element of truth [and] should give us pause for reflection." As a measuring stick, he suggested asking, "Would the RaMaZ be comfortable in our celebrations?" The grand scale, immodest attire, and undue emphasis on material pleasure at some of the more lavish events undoubtedly would have alarmed their rabbinical namesake, he contended.[13]

On several occasions over the years Rabbi Lookstein felt compelled to send Ramaz parents appeals to "emphasize the 'Mitzvah' part of the celebration rather than the 'Bar' aspect."[14] "Some celebrations that are being held may be acceptable for adults, depending upon one's preferences, but they are not appropriate for Middle School age children," he wrote. "Children do not need a dinner-dance for their bar and bat mitzvah. Children do not need a quasi wedding to celebrate their coming of age religiously ... it is inappropriate to invite children to celebrate a bar and bat mitzvah at an adult dinner party that features disco dancing and social dancing."[15]

Another major area of new responsibility for R. Haskel as senior rabbi was fundraising. Most synagogues have either a paid director of development or at least volunteer fundraisers from among the congregation. At KJ, by contrast, responsibility for fundraising has always been invested solely in the rabbi. At the time that Rabbi Lookstein took over from his father, the annual synagogue appeal raised approximately $100,000, which constituted about 20 percent of the synagogue's yearly budget. It is testimony to Rabbi Lookstein's success that by 2008 the appeal raised more than $1.5 milllion annually, representing about 40 percent of the budget. Major construction projects requiring astronomical sums have been made his responsibility: R. Haskel raised most of the $10.5 million needed to build the new upper school during 1977–1980, and all of the $35 million for the new middle school during 1998–2000. A contemplated major expansion of the lower school and synagogue in 2008–2009 will necessitate raising tens of millions.[16]

The rabbi explained his strategy for "Running a Successful Annual Synagogue Appeal" in the pages of the Rabbinical Council of America's newsletter *Resource*, in which veteran pulpit rabbis share with their younger colleagues the benefit of their experiences. "I hate fundraising," he began. "I am uncomfortable asking others to give to my shul. I get terribly anxious as the time launching the Annual Synagogue Appeal approaches." But he proceeds nonetheless, because doing so is "critical to the life of the congregation"; there is nobody more effective at the task than the rabbi, since he is [or is supposed to be] the most revered and trusted member of the community; and because if a rabbi is immersed in fundraising, lay leaders will be comfortable inviting him to play more of a role in budget and policy matters.

The secret to KJ's success, he wrote, was first that it did away with the traditional practice of holding the annual appeal at the time of the Kol Nidre service on Yom Kippur eve. "We used to do this at KJ also until the late 1940s. Then my father changed it. In the first year he doubled the results" and subsequently the returns continued to increase until by the mid-1990s they had reached close to 40 percent of KJ's budget. R. Haskel urged his colleagues to "recognize that Kol Nidre night should be devoted to prayer and repentance. Charity should not come from a mass appeal, but from a personal approach....

Spend five minutes on a silent appeal and get on with *kedushat hayom* [the sanctity of the day]."

The annual appeal process begins with the rabbi's review, each spring, of the KJ membership list, to select those who are able to give most generously. A letter is mailed to each one. It includes an invitation to a meeting in the rabbi's home and a pledge card. Some donors immediately return the card with a check; others opt to attend the meeting, which can have as many as 60 to 70 people in attendance. The majority of those who attend the first meeting make their contributions on the spot. The day after the meeting, letters go out to the pledgers, thanking them for their generosity. This same process is repeated for a second meeting. Seventy-five percent of the final total comes from the two meetings. The remainder is contributed as a result of letters and calls from the rabbi just before Rosh Hashana and Yom Kippur and then again toward the end of the calendar year.

"Jews are taught by our religion to be generous," he wrote, concluding his recommendations on an optimistic note. "Most will respond to a sincere, hardworking rabbi who has the congregation's needs at heart. A successful annual synagogue appeal will not happen overnight. It needs consistent, systematic, and energetic hard work year after year. With such an effort the results will grow, the congregation will thrive, and the Rabbi will feel his commitment of time and personal energy has been most worthwhile."[17]

## NOTES

[1] RHL, "A Milestone and the Reflections It Inspires" [sermon delivered by Rabbi Haskel Lookstein on his 10th anniversary in the rabbinate of Kehilath Jeshurun, June 15, 1968], File: Sermons, KJ. Ferziger, in "Lookstein Legacy," argued that the phenomenon of Joseph Lookstein succeeding his grandfather-in-law and then in turn being succeeded by his own son demonstrated that a "Lookstein dynasty" had taken shape. The subsequent decision of R. Haskel's son Joshua to choose a different career path demonstrated otherwise.

[2] RHL, "The Rabbi: Then and Now—A Comparison," 16 April 1960, File: Rabbi Haskel Lookstein, KJ, p. 4.

[3] Mayer Moskowitz Testimonial, 25th Anniversary Tribute Book, KJ.

[4] Ira M. Miller, "Rabbi Haskel Lookstein: A Personal Tribute," 25th Anniversary Tribute Book, KJ.

[5] Testimonial by Alexandra Pike, in "A Tribute to Rabbi Haskel Lookstein in Honor of His 70th Birthday" [New York : Kehilath Jeshurun, 2002].

[6] Testimonial by Martin Sanders, in "A Tribute to Rabbi Haskel Lookstein," op.cit.

[7] Testimonial by Bonnie and Isaac Pollak, in ibid.

[8] "Chesed Means Caring," Chavrusa [Yeshiva University Rabbinic Alumni newsletter] XVIII:2, February 1984, pp. 1–2; RHL, " 'If You Were God...' [A Rosh Hashanah Sermon]," KJB LI:2 [3 October 1983], p. 5; "Chesed Campaign Adds New Dimension to Synagogue Life," KJB LI:2 [3 October 1983], p. 4; "Massive Food Drive Set for Kol Nidre Night," KJB LVII:1 [15 September 1989], p. 2.

[9] Rabbi Haskel Lookstein, "If Menschliness Before Godliness Then Why Godliness? [Rosh Hashana 1986], Kehilath Jeshurun Bulletin LIV:4 [19 December 1986], p. 3.

[10] Ibid.

[11] Walter Ruby, "The Material Evidence Against Materialism," Jewish World 14–20 May 1999.

[12] Lang Phipps, "Mitzvah or Mania?" New York Times, 21 April 1996; Rabbi Haskel Lookstein, "Mollywood Madness—Implications for Us All" [sermon], 29 April 1996, File: Sermons, KJ.

[13] Ralph Gardner, Jr., "Bash Mitzvahs!" New York Magazine, 9 March 1998; Rabbi Haskel Lookstein, "Thank You, New York Magazine" [sermon], 7 March 1998, File: Sermons, KJ.

[14] Rabbi Haskel Lookstein to Ramaz parents, December 1982, File: Ramaz, KJ.

[15] Principal's Letter, 27 October 2004, File: Ramaz, KJ.

[16] RHL Interview, 12 February 2008.

[17] Rabbi Haskel Lookstein, "Running a Successful Annual Synagogue Appeal," Resource [RCA Newsletter, undated], KJ

# VI. THE ACTIVIST

Political or social activism was hardly the hallmark of American Orthodox rabbis in the 1960s. While a number of Conservative and Reform rabbis participated in the civil rights movement or protested U.S. involvement in the Vietnam War, their Orthodox counterparts typically regarded such causes as too far removed from Jewish concerns to justify their involvement. Haskel Lookstein, while not personally active in those battles, early on recognized a connection between traditional Jewish concepts and modern social struggles. In a May 1966 sermon, which was the subject of a sizable article in the *New York Times,* he argued that the Talmud advocated principles similar to that of the civil rights movement. "It is the Talmud that says that no man is free if he must live in a segregated community, whether that segregation is the creation of law or the result of informal social consensus," he declared. "It is the Talmud that states that no man is free unless he has economic opportunity, a chance for employment, the social possibility to work in any geographical and economic area in accordance with his God-given and acquired talents."[1] In 1971 he was one of the few Orthodox rabbis to publicly endorse Cesar Chavez's battles for the rights of farm workers, he urged his KJ members to boycott nonunion lettuce. Technically, all lettuce was kosher, he acknowledged, but lettuce produced "under exploitative conditions" should be regarded as nonkosher. Years later, during his tenure as president of the New York

Board of Rabbis, R. Haskel engineered the adoption of a resolution urging "all Rabbis and their congregants" to boycott nonunion grapes, declaring such produce to be in violation of "ethical kashrut."[2]

Although some of Rabbi Lookstein's rhetoric during that period echoed the social justice pronouncements of his non-Orthodox colleagues, he was not prepared to take an active role in the causes that interested them. In retrospect, he attributed his reluctance to both the burden of his recently assumed new responsibilities at KJ and Ramaz, and the general attitude in the Orthodox community—which he shared to some extent—that they were not "Jewish issues." As will be seen below, when an indisputably Jewish issue later emerged, Rabbi Lookstein rose to the challenge.

In the aftermath of the Communist revolution of 1917 in Russia, Jewish religious and communal life there was decimated. Most Jewish schools and synagogues were shut down, the Hebrew language and Zionist activity were banned, many prominent Jews were subjected to show trials and executed, and emigration was prohibited. Russia's Jews could neither live as Jews nor leave. Until the 1960s, the American Jewish community exhibited relatively limited interest in the treatment of Soviet Jews. This indifference was the result of a lack of information about the condition of Soviet Jewry, sympathy for the USSR because of its alliance with the United States against the Nazis, and a general reluctance to raise Jewish issues in the public arena. But a wave of show trials and Soviet government-sponsored anti-Semitism in 1963 stirred concern in the U.S. Jewish community and led to the creation of two grassroots activist groups, the Student Struggle for Soviet Jewry [SSSJ] and the Cleveland Council on Soviet Anti-Semitism. In subsequent years additional councils along the Cleveland model were established in other cities, and they came to form the Union of Councils for Soviet Jews [UCSJ]. *The Jews of Silence,* a book by Elie Wiesel about the plight of Soviet Jewry, published in 1966, also helped arouse public interest.

This protest movement gained momentum after the 1967 Six Day War, when a growing number of Soviet Jews, emboldened and inspired by Israel's victory, sought permission to emigrate to the Jewish state. In 1969 a militant approach to the issue was adopted by another grassroots U.S. protest movement, the Jewish Defense League, which advocated violence against Soviet diplomatic targets in the United States. The activities of SSSJ, UCSJ, and JDL elicited sympathy from a significant segment of American Jewry, although these groups exercised little power in the organized Jewish community. During the 1960s major Jewish organizations took only limited interest in the Soviet Jewry issue, and the American Conference on Soviet Jewry, the established groups' official mouthpiece on the issue, was provided with little in the way of resources or staff. But the activists' protests, combined with growing interest in the issue among the Jewish public, the media, and the U.S. Congress, compelled major Jewish organizations to become more involved in Soviet Jewry activity starting in the early 1970s. The American Conference on Soviet Jewry, reconstituted as the National Conference on Soviet Jewry, finally was given appropriate funding. A second organization, the Greater New York Conference on Soviet Jewry, was created by the major Jewish groups at about the same time and became the focal point for Soviet Jewry activity in the New York area, the movement's most important base of operations. The National Conference and Greater New York Conference favored a more cautious approach than the activists, often preferring quiet diplomatic contacts to public rallies.

American Orthodox Jews tended to be disproportionately involved in Soviet Jewry activism. The SSSJ's founders and leaders included R. Haskel's friends, Rabbis Shlomo Riskin, Yitz Greenberg, and Avi Weiss, and a majority of SSSJ activists in the New York City area—the group's largest branch—were students from Yeshiva University or modern Orthodox day schools such as the Manhattan Talmudic Academy [Y.U.'s high school], the Yeshiva of Flatbush, and later Ramaz.[3] Students from separatist yeshivas, however, were not a common sight at Soviet Jewry rallies; their rabbis tended to regard demonstrations as an unjustified diversion from Torah studies.[4] In addition, a minority of well-known Orthodox rabbis, such as Pinchas Teitz of

New Jersey, David Hollander of Brooklyn, and Arthur Schneier of Manhattan, claimed that public protests could result in a backlash against Soviet Jews by the Kremlin. They emphasized the value of quiet diplomacy and visits by American rabbis to Jewish communities in the USSR.

Rabbi Lookstein and KJ took an active interest in the subject early on. After the aforementioned 1964 Men's Club meeting featuring a film about Soviet Jewry, KJ's Shachar teen group held its own showing of the film and then drafted a petition of protest to the Soviet government. The following year the Men's Club hosted a presentation by Rabbinical Council of America president Rabbi Israel Miller about his recent visit to the USSR. Shortly before Pesach in 1966 the KJ newsletter featured a full-page appeal to congregants to add to their seder table "a matzah of oppression—an additional matzah which will not be eaten and which will symbolize the plight of our brethren in the Soviet Union." KJ was one of the first synagogues to adopt this practice and it helped legitimize such activities in the American Jewish community. In the fall of 1966 R. Haskel's sermon on the weekly portion of Noah compared that biblical figure's reputation for selfishness to the selfishness of "people who refrain from joining protests in behalf of three million Russian Jews for fear of aggravating relations between the United States and the Soviet Union." During the intermediate days of Passover in 1967 Ramaz set up a Soviet Jewry protest tent in front of the United Nations headquarters and held a 24-hour vigil. The following year the KJ newsletter included a clip-out petition to the U.N. Secretary General about the persecution of Soviet Jews; more than 1,000 people signed it.[5]

KJ took part in protests against the mistreatment of Jews in other countries as well. When the Iraqi government executed a group of Jews on trumped-up espionage charges in January 1969, Rabbi Lookstein responded by spearheading a large protest rally. Only a small portion of the estimated 20,000 demonstrators could fit inside Kehilath Jeshurun; the bulk of the crowd spilled into the street outside. After listening to speeches by an array of public figures ["the interfaith character [of the event] was particularly heartwarming in a city beset by tensions between various racial and economic groups," Rabbi Lookstein wrote afterwards], the protesters marched to the Iraqi Mission to the United Nations to express their outrage over the persecution of Iraqi Jewry.[6]

In view of Rabbi Lookstein's later clashes with the *New York Times* over its coverage of Israel, it is interesting to note that it was the 1969 rally for Iraqi Jews that triggered his first dispute with the *Times*. In a blistering letter to the editor [which was not published], Rabbi Lookstein took the *Times* to task for its "grossly misplaced emphasis" on a few minor skirmishes between the police and the demonstrators. In a line that foreshadowed his own skirmishes with the *Times* years later, Rabbi Lookstein wrote to the editors: "Does coverage of the news require that the reporter consistently accentuate the negative and deemphasize the positive?" The curt reply from the *Times* foreshadowed the editors' responses to the later Lookstein protests: "We are sorry to learn that you were displeased" with the *Times'* coverage of the event, "but are glad you wrote to give us your views."[7]

Rabbi Lookstein's involvement in the Soviet Jewry movement intensified in late 1970 and early 1971, after he was visited in his synagogue office by Malcolm Hoenlein, director of the nascent Greater New York Conference on Soviet Jewry. Hoenlein was recruiting young rabbis to the cause, and Rabbi Lookstein agreed to serve on the group's executive committee. During the next year a newly organized committee, Kehilath Jeshurun for Soviet Jewry, sponsored a series of activities that reflected the congregation's growing commitment to Russia's Jews. On Purim, special prayers for Soviet Jewry were added to the service. On Passover, families again added the "matzah of oppression" to their seders. In September KJ hosted a community-wide memorial service for the victims of Babi Yar, site of a Nazi massacre of Soviet Jews in 1941, featuring the leading congressional champion of Soviet Jewry, U.S. Senator Henry Jackson. R. Haskel and KJ actively promoted the Jackson-Vanik Amendment, a congressional initiative linking U.S. trade with the USSR to Jewish emigration, which helped pressure the

Soviets to permit more Jews to leave during the early 1970s. On Yom Kippur of 1971, KJ members held a prayer service for Soviet Jewry near the United Nations. Shortly before Hanukkah that year, R. Haskel urged congregants to forgo giving their children typical gifts and instead present them with tickets to the upcoming "Freedom Lights for Soviet Jewry" event at Madison Square Garden; some 500 tickets were sold through KJ and Ramaz.[8]

For Rabbi Lookstein, the turning point in his activism for Soviet Jewry came in the spring of 1972, when his friend Rabbi Louis Bernstein, president of the Rabbinical Council of America, proposed that R. Haskel travel to the Soviet Union. Bernstein himself had been to the USSR, as had R. Haskel's friend and colleague, Ramaz administrator Noam Shudofsky [together with his wife, Nechi]. They believed Rabbi Lookstein, with his outgoing personality and devotion to chesed, would be well suited to bring encouragement and spiritual succor to Russia's Jews. Rabbi Bernstein also wanted Audrey to participate, knowing from experience that a couple would be more effective than a lone rabbi. The Looksteins agreed. "I learned from my in-laws that whenever possible, the rabbi and his wife should go together to public events," Audrey noted. "From both the personal and professional point of view, it was a formula that was successful for them, and I tried to follow that example—although I couldn't have anticipated that it would mean going to the Soviet Union." With assistance from the RCA and Yehoshua Pratt, an Israeli Consular official and Ramaz parent, Rabbi and Mrs. Lookstein mapped out an itinerary that would ensure maximum interaction with refuseniks in Moscow, Leningrad, and Kiev.

They arrived in Leningrad on September 20, bringing books and religious articles [including four sets of lulavim and etrogim] to give to local Jews. They also brought a large supply of canned tuna fish and soup cubes, which would be their main source of kosher food throughout their thirteen days behind the Iron Curtain. They each lost more than fifteen pounds over the next two weeks.

Two days later, on Sukkot, the Looksteins attended services at the Leningrad Synagogue. Word of their arrival had spread quickly in the local Jewish community and more than 1,000 people attended services, no doubt some of them motivated to come because of the rare visit by a young American rabbi. Requesting the honor of reading the *haftorah*, R. Haskel proceeded to put emphasis on each word "as if I were davening *ne'ila*," he said. Officially he could not deliver a sermon in the synagogue, since he was in the Soviet Union as a tourist, not a visiting rabbi. Nonetheless, he gave what he later called "a political address via the Tanach." He chose as his subject Ezekiel's vision of the valley of the dry bones, which is normally read and discussed on Shabbat chol ha-moed rather than on Sukkot, but it struck R. Haskel as unusually relevant, given the circumstances. Speaking in Yiddish— which he had studied that summer in preparation for the trip, and to which he had also grown accustomed in Rav Soloveitchik's classes—"I said to them, 'Like those bones, you thought you were dried up, finished, but God says, "I will bring you out of your graves and plant you on your land, I promise and I will do it.""'

He and Audrey ate with members of the congregation in the synagogue's sukkah, "which looked like it would hold about 75 people, but by the second day somehow there were 300 jammed into it." He made *kiddush* and *hamotzi* for the congregation, and during the meals taught the words and tunes to various "*zmirot* of redemption," that is, Shabbat table songs with verses pertaining to the ingathering of the exiles and similar themes.

At one point Rabbi Lookstein was approached by a 96-year-old man who, upon hearing the rabbi's last name, suspected they might be related. It took only a few moments of matching relatives' names to discover that the man, Mikhail Abramovich Lokshin, was the brother of the rabbi's grandfather, Yaakov Shachna Lokshin, from the town of Simyatitch. They both had tears in their eyes as they embraced and marveled at the phenomenon of kin reuniting after so long.[9] "It was an incredibly emotional experience for everyone in that jam-packed sukkah," the rabbi noted.

In the streets outside the Leningrad synagogue the rabbi and Audrey met with several refuseniks, conversing as they strolled so as not to attract attention. [A lovers' lane near the St. Isaac's Cathedral proved useful, as the couples were "too busy with their own affairs" to pay them any mind.] While in Leningrad, they also delivered a lulav and etrog to a Lubavitcher Chassid who was too ill to come to the synagogue.

From Leningrad they traveled briefly to Kiev, "a very hostile and tightly controlled city" where, for the first time, Rabbi Lookstein realized they were being followed by a KGB agent. Meeting aliyah activists in Kiev proved complicated because the activists were denied access to the Kiev synagogue, but the rabbi was able to share with them a copy of a letter to KJ members Rosalie and Harry Kleinhaus, which refuseniks had dictated to them by telephone two weeks earlier and which had appeared in the *New York Times* the day the Looksteins left the United States. While in Kiev, the Looksteins visited the Babi Yar massacre site. The Soviets' refusal to acknowledge the Jewish identity of the victims or permit the erection of monuments on the site fueled international controversy in the late 1960s. "Babi Yar was of course a terrible disappointment," Rabbi Lookstein wrote afterwards. "There is nothing to see, which I guess is something too."[10]

The Looksteins then proceeded to Moscow for the last days of the Sukkot holiday. On chol ha-moed and Hoshana Rabba, the rabbi davened and gave classes in both of the city's synagogues. But the main event was Simchat Torah. Taking over the evening service, Rabbi Lookstein exhorted the crowd of 1,500—twice the number that normally filled the synagogue—to sing and dance. A *Washington Post* correspondent who was on hand reported:

> Inside the temple, the singing and dancing was encouraged by an American rabbi, Rev. Haskel Lookstein of New York City. He repeatedly tried to arouse the congregation to sing more loudly, remarking that Jews in New York were trying to sing loud enough to be heard in Russia and asking the Moscow Jews to reciprocate in kind.[11]

The crowd responded with enthusiasm. "They were waiting for an experience, and the synagogue establishment was simply not capable of giving it to them," he wrote. "I therefore tried my best, with some pretty good results."[12] Those results were repeated the next morning, when a comparably huge crowd, some of them undoubtedly attracted by word of the previous night's celebration, erupted in prolonged singing and dancing. Yearning to reconnect to their Jewish roots and inspired by an American rabbi who had come thousands of miles to be part of their lives, the Jews of Moscow turned that Simchat Torah into an event of a lifetime—for themselves and for Rabbi Lookstein. "In going around the synagogue, I was able to shake hands with hundreds of Jews who whispered their words of encouragement, hope, warning, prayer, etc., to me," he recounted. "Of course, I tried to respond to each in an individual way."[13]

The Looksteins' final days in Moscow, after Yom Tov, were spent meeting with Jewish activists, in particular the family of Roman Rutman, for whom, remarkably, the rabbi conducted both a conversion and a wedding. Rabbi Lookstein brought Rutman a siddur, tallis, tefillin, and Jewish books that he smuggled into the USSR, and he spent hours teaching him how to pray, recite grace after meals, observe Shabbat, and keep kosher. Rutman's wife, Lena, considered herself a Jew but had a non-Jewish mother, so Rabbi Lookstein organized a conversion ceremony at the mikveh of the Moscow synagogue and then, immediately afterwards, conducted a Jewish wedding for them in their home. Numerous prominent activists and refuseniks filled the tiny apartment although, in a reminder of grim reality, one of their closest friends, Vladimir Slepak, could not attend because he was in prison for seeking to emigrate. Rabbi Lookstein left the Rutmans with a tape recording of the Shabbat prayer services and assorted *zmirot*. In his subsequent report to the Rabbinical Council of America on his trip, R. Haskel noted that in addition to their well-publicized desire to emigrate, "their willingness as students points up a very serious interest on the part of many of these activists in growing Jewishly and expanding their Jewish education and experience."[14] The Looksteins left Moscow "under very close surveillance," and some of their rolls of film were confiscated by a customs officer who, oddly enough, spoke fluent Hebrew as well as English.[15]

In choosing Rabbi Lookstein for the mission, the RCA leadership secured for itself a meticulous reporter with a keen eye for detail. This characteristic was important, because the Soviet regime's tight controls made it impossible for the outside Jewish world to receive anything but the sketchiest of information about Soviet Jewish life in general, or about the needs of the activists and refuseniks in particular. Upon his return from the USSR, the rabbi composed a highly detailed, four-teen-page, single-spaced memorandum not only chronicling his experiences but providing specific, practical advice on how future shlichim should conduct themselves.

He offered crucial guidance for making one's way through the labyrinth of synagogue officials in each city, who ranged from sincere-ly pious to paid agents of the KGB. Visitors would need to know, for example, that at the main Moscow synagogue, Motel the Shochet was "quite trustworthy," but Shmuel the Shochet, he cautioned, was "less trustworthy." Reb Sholem is "a brilliant *lamdan*" who once tutored Rabbi Joseph Soloveitchik; but Ephraim Kaplun, who runs the syna-gogue, "is a big *am ha-aretz* [ignoramus]," and if he were given reli-gious articles for distribution to the needy, he would sell them on the black market for wildly inflated prices.[16]

Rabbi Lookstein's report also included precise directions for find-ing the synagogues in each city; detailed advice on how to relate to the synagogue officials ["Try to make friends immediately with the heads of the synagogue; indicate that you have heard a great deal about their work and you value it greatly"]; a list of what type and quantity of religious articles to bring, how to distribute them ["noth-ing whatsoever should be given to any official in any synagogue—it is absolutely like throwing it in the trash basket, or worse"], and how to pack them so as not to attract attention from customs officials [in the middle of the suitcase, equidistant from all sides]; a list of kosher nonperishable foods to bring along "in order that one should not starve in the Soviet Union"; how to smuggle messages out of the USSR, and tips on reducing the likelihood that customs officials will scrutinize one's luggage on the way out, such as "stalling with exchanging currency back into dollars, so that there is very little time left for the examination of baggage"; and suggestions on how to persuade nervous synagogue officials to permit conversion ceremonies at the mikvah ["a few rubles will go a long way toward getting their silence"] and how to perform weddings under unusual circumstances [for example, "memorize the *ketuba* [religious marriage contract] before you go to the Soviet Union"]. He also included advice on how a visiting couple might maximize the fact that there are two of them, such as walking separately to and from the synagogue in order to speak with twice as many people, and standing on separate lines at customs in order to determine which officials were less scrupulous.[17]

Finally, Rabbi Lookstein's report stressed a significant point that departed somewhat from the public emphasis on the issue of emigration: while the main goal of Russian Jews was to leave the USSR, "they do not know when their ultimate goal of aliyah will be reached." Thus "it is necessary for them to live a little bit for the present as well. They want to deepen their Jewish experience beyond the purely national and social....They hunger for God and religion; we must help to satisfy that hunger." The struggle for Soviet Jewry, he argued, needed to take place on two levels simultaneously: an international political battle for the right to emigrate, and a more personal campaign, within the Soviet Union, to bring Jewish knowledge and practice to individuals while they wait—often for years—for exit permits. The visiting rabbi and rebbitzen must be prepared to "go to the homes of activists and spend long periods of time with a family or a small group," teaching them basic Judaism. "Much can be accomplished even in a matter of days, and future visitors can follow up on the initial education which is given."[18]

Rabbi and Mrs. Lookstein themselves accomplished much in their sixteen days behind the Iron Curtain. Their willingness to undertake such an arduous journey boosted the morale of a downtrodden community that had been virtually cut off from the outside world for more than half a century. Rabbi Lookstein's take-charge personality energized and inspired the Simchat Torah crowds. In their private meetings with Soviet Jews and in the classes that the rabbi gave in the synagogues, the Looksteins shared Jewish knowledge with eager audiences. They also collected valuable information about the plight of individual aliyah activists for use in the American Jewish community's battle for the right to emigrate. And they provided their sponsor, the Rabbinical Council of America, with an invaluable eyewitness account to help guide future emissaries.

As much as the trip accomplished for Soviet Jews, Rabbi Lookstein looked back upon it as an experience that affected him just as deeply:

> The visit was a turning point in my life. Before we left the U.S., my uncle, Bernard Fishman, said to me, "Hack, make the most of this trip because it will change your life. You will never be the same after it. What you experience will have a profound impact on you for the rest of your rabbinic career and your personal life." He couldn't have been more accurate. I truly began to feel that it was my responsibility to help Jews wherever they might be.[19]

The journey to the USSR in 1972 transformed R. Haskel into a deeply committed activist for Soviet Jewry. While he had felt concern for Russia's Jews prior to the journey, now their situation seemed much more real, and urgent. He saw, up close, the all-enveloping atmosphere of intimidation in which Jews lived. He was followed by the KGB. He was strip-searched at the airport. His film had been confiscated for no reason. After this brief, bitter taste of life for Jews in Russia, he was no longer content to adopt the stance of the typical American rabbi, sympathetic but too busy with other responsibilities to become more than tangentially involved in an ongoing protest movement. Rabbi Lookstein now felt connected to Soviet Jewry in a profoundly personal way. Every time he read in the newspapers about the plight of a refusenik or a harsh new Soviet decree, he connected it to his own powerful memories of people and places that he had seen firsthand.

The congregants at KJ and the students and faculty at Ramaz soon learned that the Soviet Jewry struggle was not some flash-in-the-pan cause for their rabbi but rather reflected a profound commitment that he had undertaken, and which he fervently hoped they would share. In a letter to KJ members shortly after his return, Rabbi Lookstein reported that "it would be an understatement to say that these were the most important, inspiring, and productive days in our entire lives.... Our experience has drastically changed our lives. Perhaps it can have an effect on yours as well." He and Audrey subsequently provided a full report on their trip to a standing-room-only audience in the KJ auditorium.[20]

In the weeks and months that followed, Rabbi Lookstein and Noam Shudofsky initiated a series of projects that moved the Soviet Jewry issue to the top of the agenda of both the synagogue and the school, while simultaneously bringing it to wider public attention as well. KJ's "Kehilath Jeshurun for Soviet Jewry" committee was now rejuvenated and helped implement the new projects. The first was a rally by yeshiva students near the United Nations, to coincide with International Human Rights Day. Although conceived and to a large extent organized by Rabbi Lookstein, he realized that the students' protest would be far more effective if it took place under the auspices of mainstream Jewish organizations. He also understood that partnering with the established Jewish leadership, which was sometimes reluctant to engage in street rallies, could help redefine the communal consensus as to what kind of protest tactics were acceptable. At his request, the Greater New York Conference on Soviet Jewry agreed to serve as the main sponsor of the students' rally.[21] This episode illustrates the unique role that R. Haskel was beginning to assume in the Soviet Jewry movement. He was a Jewish leader who embraced activist tactics yet operated from within the established Jewish leadership. By doing so, he helped make activism a legitimate part of the Jewish agenda by bringing to it the imprimatur of the Jewish establishment while at the same time leading large numbers of KJ members and Ramaz students to become activists.

At the synagogue, Rabbi Lookstein sought to ensure, first and foremost, that Soviet Jewry was always on the minds of his congregants. It soon became difficult to walk into the Kehilath Jeshurun building without being reminded of their plight, thanks to the uniquely redesigned bulletin board on the front of the building. Routine information about upcoming events was moved down, and the top half of the marquee was devoted to a message pertaining to Russia's Jews. "It's human nature to forget last month's news," the rabbi explained. "My goal was to keep the issue in front of the people all the time."[22] The messages on the board, which would change periodically, highlighted a particular Soviet Jew by name and announced the number of months since he or she was first denied the right to emigrate, or a similar statistic. When Natan Sharansky was sentenced to thirteen years in prison in 1977, the bulletin board began to note the number of Shabbats in which he had been imprisoned and how many more he had to go. That message remained, with the number updated weekly, until Sharansky was released eight and a half years later. "It was not very hard to have such a bulletin board, and it helped keep the tragedy in the forefront of the minds of the Jewish community," according to Rabbi Lookstein. "It was exactly the kind of thing I wrote about in my book—the sort of thing that American synagogues should have done during the Holocaust, but didn't." Soon after becoming president of the New York Board of Rabbis in 1979, Rabbi Lookstein sent an appeal from the Board to rabbis throughout the city, complete with a photograph of the KJ marquee, urging them to do something similar at their synagogues.[23]

During the services themselves, references to the plight of Soviet Jewry became commonplace. An extra psalm was added at the end of every *shacharit* service as an expression of solidarity with Russia's Jews, and after becoming president of the RIETS Alumni Association in 1982, R. Haskel urged attendees at the group's annual convention to do likewise in their own synagogues. The Chicago Rabbinical Council quickly adopted the proposal, as did other agencies and synagogues.[24] Rabbi Lookstein, together with Rabbi Joshua Bakst, headmaster of the Ramaz Upper School, composed a "Prayer for Soviet Jews," in Hebrew and English, which was added to KJ's Yizkor service booklet. The prayer asked God to rescue "the remnant of Thy people who are victims of repression and persecution in the Soviet Union." Significantly, nearly half of the seventeen-line prayer focused not on Soviet Jewry but on the need for activism by Jews abroad and the positive impact such activism had on American Jews. "Strengthen our resolve to stand in solidarity with them, to strive for their deliverance, and to struggle for their freedom," the prayer pleaded. "Help us to understand that as we dedicate our efforts for their redemption we simultaneously redeem ourselves. The battle for their survival ... raises our sense of purpose, uplifts our lives, and gives noble meaning to our existence."[25]

The idea that Soviet Jewry protests helped not only the refuseniks but the protesters themselves was both an unexpected benefit of the movement and an indication of how central a role the Soviet Jewry cause had come to play in the lives of many KJ members. Rabbi Lookstein perceived the Soviet Jewry struggle not merely as an occasional activity alongside numerous other activities in his congregants' daily routines, but rather as a core part of their lives as Jews. Moreover, Soviet Jewry activism also infused younger Jews with a sense of confidence that they might otherwise lack. "I remember taking part in a march down Fifth Avenue around 1973," R. Haskel said. "At about 55th Street, as the marchers passed a church, I heard two of my daughters, who were in sixth or seventh grade and were marching in the front, chanting, 'We are Jews, we couldn't be prouder, and if you can't hear us, we'll yell a little louder!' I thought to myself, 'What a difference between now and when I grew up.' In the 1930s and 1940s, when we carried our Hebrew books to school, we would hold them with the covers facing inward so nobody would see were Jews." At Ramaz in those days, R. Joseph insisted that a yarmulke be regarded as an "indoor garment," to the point that students reportedly were told to remove their yarmulkes before exiting the building during fire drills, reflecting an attitude that was not uncommon among American Orthodox Jews.[26]

"My father used to say, 'In the 1940s we walked around like question marks, bent over'—but in the 1970s, we were starting to walk around like exclamation points," R. Haskel noted. "The Soviet Jewry movement played a major part in bringing about that change, along with other factors such as the Six Day War and the ethnic pride movements among blacks and other minorities. They said 'Black is beautiful!' We were starting to think, 'Jewish is beautiful too!'"[27]

Many former refuseniks who visited the United States spoke from the KJ pulpit. Eliahu Essas, Roman Rutman, Vladimir Slepak and Alexander Luntz were among the synagogue's guest speakers on Shabbat or Yom Tov. On the High Holidays a large poster of a refusenik would be placed on a chair next to the ark. "I would speak about the person on the poster and express my hope and faith that one day he or she would be there to join us," Rabbi Lookstein said. "We had a poster of Sharansky there a number of times and spoke about him. I was convinced that one day the poster would be gone and Sharansky himself would be sitting there."

Rabbi Lookstein first met Sharansky when he and Audrey returned to the USSR for Sukkot in September 1975, again under the auspices of the Rabbinical Council of America. They were accompanied by Mario Merola, district attorney of the Bronx. Jewish organizations often sought to include U.S. political figures on such trips, both to sensitize officeholders to the plight of Soviet Jewry and to put additional pressure on the Soviets.

It turned out to be "an extraordinary trip," in fact "much more productive even than our first one, which we thought it would be impossible to equal." The second time around, "you not only know what to do but you are also received with greater enthusiasm by the Jews."[28] The most remarkable difference between the first trip and the second, the rabbi and Audrey immediately discovered, was the increased pride and boldness of the refuseniks. Whereas in 1972 the atmosphere was almost completely one of fear, now they found that while the fear was not gone, there was also "confidence ... the conviction of these people that they were doing the right thing and that in the not too distant future they would be reunited with their people in the land of Israel." He described the refuseniks they met in 1975 as "the only free people in the Soviet Union." They were, he wrote, the only ones who are not intimidated by the "System." They have contempt for the KGB and its mission. They walk freely in the streets speaking Hebrew and English. They speak without hesitation in their apartments except when they are saying something which is politically very sensitive or strategically significant. I had the feeling as I walked with them through the Soviet Union that the blessing of *zokef kfufim* ["He who helps the bent stand straight"] had already been realized for these heroic individuals. They are no longer bowed. They stand upright for Israel, for Judaism, and for the Jewish People.[29]

As they did previously, the Looksteins began their mission in Leningrad, where they were still widely remembered. At the Leningrad synagogue, and outside it, they were frequently greeted, in Yiddish, Hebrew, or English, with comments such as "You didn't forget us," "Thank you for coming back," "Come again next year," and "Let's come together again next year and be together—but not here!" Rabbi Haskel's great–uncle, Mikhail Abramovich Lokshin, whom he had met in the Leningrad synagogue in 1972, was there, too —"now three months away from his 100th birthday." Once again the rabbi read the *haftorah* on Yom Tov, putting special emphasis on all references to Jerusalem. His uncle, with tears streaming down his cheeks, stood next to him at the *bima* throughout the reading. More than 1,500 people attended, some 300 of whom crowded around the *bima* to be closer to Rabbi Lookstein and be part of the experience of hearing this American Jewish leader bring them words of hope for redemption.[30] R. Haskel made *kiddush* and *ha-motzi* in the overcrowded sukkah, and during the meal led the hundreds of congregants in singing *zmirot*. As he did in 1972, he offered comments on Ezekiel's dry bones vision, but this time speaking more explicitly about Soviet Jews being set free and reaching Israel. At one point Audrey spotted six men who appeared to be KGB agents entering the courtyard, with two of them staying to listen to his talk in Yiddish. She quickly signaled the rabbi to cut his remarks short. "Fortunately, my Yiddish is so inadequate that in retrospect I don't believe they understood my speech," he said later. "Nevertheless, it was a frightening experience."[31] They experienced another apparent encounter with the KGB later on in the trip, in Riga. Believing they had been followed while walking back to their hotel one afternoon, and suspicious that the KGB might be eavesdropping, they began writing notes to each other in the room instead of speaking. After a while, there was a knock at the door, and a man claiming he had to repair something, removed and inspected a part on the window sill. The Looksteins suspected that the KGB, knowing they were in the room but not hearing any voices, thought that the listening device they planted in the room was not working.[32]

After meeting with his Soviet counterparts to press them on the plight of Soviet Jewry, District Attorney Merola joined the Looksteins for a meeting with refuseniks in a Leningrad apartment. Merola "listened intently" as they described their experiences, R. Haskel recalled. "It is one thing for them to tell it to an American rabbi and quite another for them to tell it to an Italian Catholic district attorney who they feel carries some weight in American governmental circles. This may very well have been the most significant role that Mr. Merola filled during his visit to the Soviet Union."

The discussion introduced the Looksteins to an important new problem facing Soviet Jewry: the growing number of Jewish émigrés choosing to go to the United States instead of Israel. About 40 percent of all Soviet Jews were "dropping out," and the rates had reached 70 percent among Jews from Leningrad and Moscow. These activists feared that the Soviet authorities were intentionally giving visas only to Jews whom they believed would go to America. Their doing so would enable the Kremlin to completely shut off Jewish emigration, with international acquiescence, by claiming that the high rate of emigration to the United States proved it was "not a humanitarian matter but rather an emigration of a bunch of selfish Jews who do not like Communism and who would rather live in the rich lands of the West." This unexpected problem would vex Soviet Jewry activists in the United States in the years to follow.[33]

Several nights later the Looksteins enjoyed Shemini Atzeret dinner in the Moscow home of refusenik Vladimir Slepak, with a number of fellow activists on hand, among them Natan Sharansky. Years later Sharansky recalled how, at that first meeting, R. Haskel taught him how to do the ritual washing of the hands before a meal [*netilat yadayim*] and say the appropriate blessing. "What was so unusual was not the *bracha* itself, but rather his way of teaching it to me—as though he were a young, innocent child, excited by a newly acquired knowledge and eager to share this knowledge with another person."[34] Sharansky had another vivid memory of his first meeting with Rabbi Lookstein: a lecture in which R. Haskel spoke about Jewish heroes in ancient times. "He explained that Jewish heroes, as opposed to Greek heroes, were portrayed at times as physically weak, people full of doubts and uncertainties, but that they always prevailed because of their will, determination, and soul. This message, presented during an underground meeting of Jewish refuseniks, definitely struck home."[35] For his part, Rabbi Lookstein was impressed by Sharansky's ability to follow the lecture, which was lengthy, dealt with complex ideas, and was delivered in advanced Hebrew. "Yet it was clear from the many questions Sharansky asked me afterwards that he understood the lecture precisely," he said. Sharansky's wife, Avital, had been forced to leave the USSR the day after their wedding in 1974 and in Israel was beginning to embrace religious observance. "He told me that he had been receiving letters from Avital that contained references to the philosophy of Rav Kook, and he did not understand what she was saying," R. Haskel recalled. "I told him not to worry about learning Rav Kook's philosophy, he had more basic aspects of Judaism to learn, and he could always deal with Rav Kook at some later point."

Over the course of the next few days R. Haskel and Sharansky began what would become a close and long-lasting friendship. They spent four to five hours together each day for three days in a row, at one point walking for about three miles together, from one side of Moscow to the other, as they conversed.[36]

It was standard practice for emissaries to the USSR, on the last day of their trip, to leave their personal tallit and tefillin behind for a Soviet Jew to use. Rabbi Lookstein gave his to Sharansky. Since Sharansky had not embraced religious observance, he replied frankly that he could not promise he would put them on. R. Haskel was not fazed. "I said to him, 'Maybe you'll want to put them on tomorrow, or maybe next week, or in a year, or when you get to Israel. But whatever the case, I would be honored if you would take them. He gave in." Rabbi Lookstein also gave him a copy of *The Jewish Catalog* [a 1970s how-to book about basic Jewish practice and culture], which included a diagram of how to don tefillin, but thought it would be helpful if he also showed him directly how to do it. "When he had them on, he looked positively angelic, I just had to take a photo of him," he recalled. "Later I showed it to Zeesy Schnur, director of the Greater New York Conference on Soviet Jewry. I had no idea she was going to blow it up and make it into a poster for the next Solidarity Sunday rally."[37]

In his later description of that evening at the Slepaks' apartment, R. Haskel wrote, "I allowed myself to eat the bread so that I could teach them how to wash, make *ha-motzi* and *bensch*." Before the Looksteins' earlier trip, RCA officials had explained that they were guided by a halakhic ruling according to which in the entire period of such a mission to the USSR the rabbi should consider himself to be in a situation of *pikuach nefesh* [i.e., lives are in danger, so he can transgress certain commandments in order to help them] or at least *pidyon shvuyim* [redemption of captives, which similarly justifies briefly transgressing halakhic obligations].

In this instance, R. Haskel opted to partake of bread that was not certifiably kosher, for the sake of the higher immediate objective of teaching the refuseniks mitzvahs that they would observe for years to come. Rabbi Lookstein could have declined to eat the bread, but doing that would have both undermined his ability to teach them about the relevant laws and also caused his hosts and their friends considerable embarrassment by in effect declaring that their food was not kosher. In another instance affected by this principle, the Looksteins both carried their passports with them on Shabbat, even though there was no eruv, because they were in a dangerous situation in which an American passport could prove critical to their safety.[38]

In the meantime, the Looksteins experienced another unforgettable Simchat Torah in the USSR. The scene at the Moscow synagogue was remarkable:

Outside of the synagogue we saw 10,000 young people dancing in the streets. They started at 6:00 P.M. and did not finish until midnight. The sight had to be seen to be believed. Every place we looked they were singing and dancing and talking and simply identifying with Judaism. Needless to say, we lost our voices within 20 minutes trying to teach melodies and sing together with them outside.

Aliyah activist Alexander Luntz later recalled how Rabbi Lookstein "stood in front of the Moscow synagogue and spoke loudly on behalf of the State of Israel—something that most of those who visited us from the Free World (and, unfortunately, many Soviet Jews those days) were afraid to do. Moral support, in our struggle with the KGB, that's what we needed most, and Haskel was very good at that."[39]

After Yom Tov, the Looksteins "took a cab to God knows where and ended up at the apartment of Ina and Yuli Kosharovsky," who, like most Soviet Jews, had been married in a civil ceremony. Now they wanted to be married under a *chuppah*, with R. Haskel officiating and 75 refuseniks participating in a Jewish wedding for the first time in their lives. "Imagine my chagrin—and terror—when I discovered that both the bride and groom had been previously married. There was no possibility of obtaining a religious divorce in Moscow. A Jewish wedding was virtually out of the question, but how was I going to explain this to a group of activists who could not possibly understand my 'technical' considerations?" After further questioning, however, Rabbi Lookstein discovered, "to my absolute delight," that Ina's first husband had died and Yuli's first wife was not Jewish, thus making a Jewish divorce unnecessary. He wrote a *ketuba* from memory and proceeded to conduct the wedding with a bottle of Carmel wine that the rabbi had brought with him to Russia "just in case." "We sang and we danced for about a half hour. ....[T]here wasn't a dry eye in that room."

At a shiur the following night, refusenik Mark Asbel introduced Rabbi Lookstein by referring to the Kosharovsky wedding. "I am 43 years old," he said, "and last night was the greatest experience in my entire life—to witness a *chuppah* ceremony, to be with a rabbi who would sing with us, dance with us, and feel with us, was an unforgettable experience." Asbel presented the Looksteins with "a simple Russian art object, on the back of which all of the refuseniks who were at the wedding had signed their names, and he invited the additional refuseniks who were in the seminar on Monday night to do likewise.... That art object is the most precious possession we have in our home."[40] Another young activist who attended the wedding was Eliahu Essas, who at the time was completely nonobservant. Speaking at KJ many years later, Essas said that as he left the wedding together with several friends, "We were so moved by the experience that we said to each other, 'There must be something very powerful in this religion, something that is worth learning more about.'" Essas would go on to become not only a *ba'al teshuva*, but also the leader of a large and influential ba'al teshuva movement inside the Soviet Union.[41]

The Looksteins arrived at the airport for their flight home together with District Attorney Merola, whose presence, they assumed, would afford them a certain amount of protection against aggressive searches by the Soviet customs officials. What happened, however, is that Merola, as a government official, was quickly waved through customs without inspection. He proceeded to board the plane, not realizing that the Looksteins were receiving very different treatment. "The customs people were waiting for us," the rabbi recalled. "They took apart every piece of material in our suitcases, looking for God knows what. Of course they found nothing, but they did succeed in making us miss our plane." The wait for the next flight was four and a half hours. As the frustrated couple could do nothing but "sit around feeling sorry for ourselves," R. Haskel recalled, "I suddenly began to cry. Audrey asked me why. I told her, 'Here we are crying because we have a four hour wait to get out. Just seven hours ago we left people who have been waiting five and a half years to get out.'"42

Under Rabbi Lookstein's leadership, the Kehilath Jeshurun for Soviet Jewry committee undertook a wide range of activities, some public and others behind the scenes. Committee members made regular telephone calls to individual Jews in the USSR, to boost their morale and find out the latest information about visa denials, imprisonments, and supplies that were needed. Op-ed pieces and letters to the editor were submitted to the press. Members of Congress and professional associations were lobbied. Packages of clothing, reading materials, and other permitted items were mailed to refuseniks, while articles that could not be sent through the postal system were given to tourists to smuggle into the USSR. A telegram bank barraged Soviet officials with protest messages. Funds were raised for a variety of purposes, from over $30,000 to send Alan Dershowitz and Nuremberg prosecutor Telford Taylor to the Soviet Union to aid prisoners of conscience, to a sum of several thousand dollars that was used to ransom a Russian Jew. Cultural activities were also undertaken, such as sponsoring performances of Elie Wiesel's play *Zalmen*, about Soviet Jews, and supporting a ballet recital by two former refuseniks.[43]

The committee was also in charge of mobilizing the KJ-Ramaz community to take part in the Greater New York Conference's annual "Solidarity Sunday with Soviet Jewry" march through midtown Manhattan. In a typical year 500 or more people assembled in front of KJ and then walked to Fifth Avenue to join the tens of thousands of protesters in the main march.

In the summer of 1979 the Greater New York Conference asked Rabbi Lookstein to chair the following year's event. As associate chairman of the Greater New York Conference, R. Haskel had played an important role in previous Solidarity Sundays, particularly in the area of mobilizing day school principals to send their students to the march. His Conference colleagues also remembered, with appreciation, how he persuaded prominent Manhattan rabbis to withdraw their synagogues' advertisements from the *New York Times* for one month to protest the *Times'* decision to relegate its coverage of the 1976 Solidarity Sunday rally to page 61.[44]

Accepting the Conference's invitation to chair the 1980 march, Rabbi Lookstein, with his characteristic attention to detail, oversaw the long series of meetings, strategy sessions, kickoffs, publicity events, and other preparatory work that preceded each year's march. The 1980 effort "did not begin so auspiciously," he later noted. "Apathy was high in almost every community and organization" because of the absence of any specific new crisis to which Solidarity Sunday could be a response. Indeed, as work began in the autumn of 1979 for the next year's rally, the number of Jews permitted to leave the USSR reached an all-time high, in response to the unrelenting pressure of the American protesters and the Kremlin's desire to improve its public image in advance of the 1980 Olympic games in Moscow. The relaxation of emigration restrictions soon proved to be temporary, however, and Solidarity Sunday's sponsors made headway with an intensive publicity campaign that included radio spots by Barbra Streisand and Judd Hirsch, solidarity resolutions in the U.S. Congress and New York State legislature, speaking tours by former refuseniks, and an all-night teach-in by spirited teens from Young Judea. Overcoming both a two-week transit strike and inclement weather on the day of the march, these efforts generated a crowd of 75,000 to 100,000, crowning a year of high-level Soviet Jewry awareness and protest activity in the run-up to the rally.[45]

Not surprisingly, the Greater New York Conference prevailed upon Rabbi Lookstein to chair the 1981 march as well, and it proved even more successful than the previous year's event, in part because R. Haskel maintained a detailed accounting of the strengths and weaknesses of the previous year's effort. His notes from 1980, and the way in which he utilized them the following year, mimic almost precisely his style of management at Kehilath Jeshurun, where the pros and cons of a particular adult education course or an Israel Independence Day program are carefully recorded in memos from the rabbi to himself and then trotted out the next time around to ensure that mistakes are not repeated. "Youth comprise a large percentage of the audience each year," one of his memos pointed out. "How can we make the program more attractive to them?" The suggestions that followed clearly reflected R. Haskel's success at infusing the Ramaz School with Soviet Jewry content. The list included placing an empty chair for a Prisoner of Zion at every school assembly; posting Soviet Jewry-related announcements on all school bulletin boards; organizing a Soviet Jewry poster contest; and inviting former refuseniks to speak to the students.[46]

Ramaz high school students embraced Soviet Jewry activism early and vigorously. Possessed of the natural idealism of youth, inclined toward activism because of their principal's ethos of chesed and social concerns, and fortuitously situated just eleven blocks from the main Soviet diplomatic office in New York, the Soviet Mission to the United Nations, Ramaz high schoolers quickly became the vanguard of student activism for the Jews of the USSR.

To facilitate his students' participation in Soviet Jewry activities, Rabbi Lookstein implemented a policy that was most unusual in the day school world: he canceled classes whenever there was a major rally. "The educational value of this active performance by the children will transcend in importance anything that they can possibly learn that day," he once explained. "If there is any meaning to the word[s] *lo ha-midrash ikar ele ha-ma'aseh* [the real point of learning is to act], it surely would refer to an act of this kind."[47] As Natan Sharansky later put it, "Demonstrations and rallies were part of the Ramaz curriculum."[48] "Other schools would send home permission slips for the parents to let their kids go to the zoo," Dean of Admissions Danièle Gorlin Lassner recalled. "We would send home permission slips to go to demonstrations." Solidarity Sunday "was practically a required school day," one student remembered.[49]

R. Haskel made no bones about his conviction that his students' participation in a Soviet Jewry demonstration was more important than the Torah learning they would have been doing during that time. In one 1972 letter to day school principals urging them to bring their students to a Soviet Jewry demonstration, Rabbi Lookstein did not argue that the rally was a one-time diversion from regular studies justified only by a particular emergency; rather, he asserted that the demonstration would make a "maximal contribution" not only to the cause of Soviet Jewry but also "to the image of Yeshiva education."[50] In the rabbi's view, the prevalent image of day schools as insular and uninterested in the world around them was unfortunate. Participation in the rally would demonstrate a social conscience and a level of concern about other Jews that R. Haskel feared was often lacking in the Orthodox community. From his perspective, activism in support of Soviet Jewry was itself a positive Jewish value and therefore precisely what day school educators should encourage, even at the occasional expense of other schoolwork or classes.[51]

When the Greater New York Conference staged a "Shofars for Freedom" ceremony near the United Nations, Ramaz students did much of the shofar-blowing. When the mayor of Moscow visited New York, Ramaz students wearing prison uniforms set up tables near the United Nations and ate a meal of hard bread and water, to demonstrate the diet Soviet Jewish prisoners endured. When a Soviet art exhibit came to the Metropolitan Museum of Art, 700 Ramaz students from grades one through twelve rallied outside. When the Moscow Circus performed at the Felt Forum, Ramaz students dressed as clowns, acrobats, and Soviet Jewish prisoners in cages staged a mock circus in front of the building.[52]

Daily life in Ramaz was permeated by the Soviet Jewry struggle. Students recall an atmosphere of "eating, sleeping, and breathing Soviet Jewry all year round."

The hallways were plastered with posters of refuseniks. Former Prisoners of Zion spoke at the school. A special plea for Soviet Jews was added to the *birkat ha-mazon* [Grace After Meals]. Referring to the latter, R. Haskel once wrote, "It is all part of consciousness raising. This is the very thing that Jews did not do during the Holocaust."[53]

"I was 14 years old [and a student at Ramaz] when [Rabbi Lookstein] came back from the Soviet Union and told us about a brave man named Anatoly Sharansky," alumnus Rivka Rosenwein later wrote in the *Wall Street Journal.* "My first consciously political act was to attend a rally on behalf of him and other 'refuseniks.'"

> My friends and I learned grass-roots politics through annual lob-
> bying trips to Washington and letter-writing campaigns to con-
> gressmen, ambassadors and three presidents. ... My high school
> graduating class voted unanimously to dedicate its yearbook to
> Anatoly Sharansky.[54]

"Sharansky Day" at Ramaz in March 1978 provided a snapshot of the role that the Soviet Jewry cause had come to play in Ramaz. To mark the one-year anniversary of Sharansky's imprisonment, all class-es and activities highlighted Sharansky's plight. The 400 students in the high school fasted for the entire day, and even the elementary schoolers undertook a partial fast. In French class, students learned the French words for "granting a pardon" and studied the original French version of a statement by Elie Wiesel about the persecution of Soviet Jewry. In English class, the students read poems about imprisonment in various countries. In their Judaic Studies classes, the Ramaz stu-dents focused on such subjects as communal fasts in response to crises, Psalms that relate to human suffering, the halakhot of redeeming cap-tives, and the obligation of a Jew to help fellow Jews. Social Studies classes compared the persecution of Jews in the USSR to the treatment of other religious minorities there, the diet given to Soviet prisoners, and due process in the Soviet legal system. Many students spent part of the day—and two additional days—on nearby street corners, gath-ering signatures on petitions in support of Sharansky. In an address to a student assembly, Rabbi Lookstein pointed out that during the Holocaust many American Jews had carried on "business as usual" despite the plight of European Jewry; he praised the Ramaz students for their very different response. The school day concluded with an address by Avital Sharansky.[55]

The most extraordinary chapter in the history of Ramaz and the Soviet Jewry struggle unfolded in the autumn of 1982. Frustrated that Sharansky "was dying in prison without even a voice being raised in his behalf," Rabbi Lookstein conceived a new plan for attracting attention to Sharansky's plight. He explained to a series of school assemblies that each day, one class in the high school would fast during the day and spend their lunch hour davening in front of the Soviet Mission. The money saved by the school on the food would pay for small weekly advertisements in the *New York Times* about Sharansky's plight. "While Jews suffer, our lives cannot simply go on as usual," he implored them. After one of the assemblies, juniors Leonard Silverman and Andrew Lassner approached the rabbi with an idea of their own: in addition to the afternoon service, they wanted to have a minyan at the Soviet Mission every morning at 7:30. "The idea sounded interesting," Rabbi Lookstein recalled, "but I didn't know whether I could impose this additional burden on the students." Privately the rabbi was somewhat skeptical, noting such inconveniences as having to bring a Torah scroll and table every Monday and Thursday. He and other faculty and administration members could take turns joining them so there would always be an adult in charge, but if Leonard and Andrew wanted to pursue it, they would have to recruit the students. They did. When the first minyan was held the next day, 21 students took part. The following day there were 33, and by the third time there were 50. Day after day, rain or shine, students walked from Ramaz to the Soviet Mission for the shacharit service.

On the twenty-fourth day, Avital Sharansky, who was visiting New York City briefly for meetings and protests, joined the students. Until that point the police guarding the Mission had chosen not to interfere with the daveners, even though a city ordinance prohibited demonstrations on that block earlier than 9:00 A.M. For whatever reason, on the twenty-fourth day the police decided to enforce the law. Right in the middle of the *Shemoneh Esrei* prayer, when Jewish law prohibits any movement of one's feet, the police captain announced that all the participants were under arrest. Rabbi Lookstein employed his best stalling tactics in order to give the students time to finish the *Shemoneh Esrei* and in anticipation of the arrival of a camera crew from the local ABC-TV affiliate, which had indicated it would cover that day's prayers since Avital Sharansky was on hand. They did arrive just in time, and with cameras rolling, the Ramaz students finished their service by reciting two special Psalms for Sharansky. Still wearing their taleisim and tefillin, Rabbi Lookstein, Ramaz teacher David Bernstein, and 65 students, all under arrest, were marched down the block to a nearby police station.

R. Haskel himself had been arrested on one prior occasion: in 1976 he, together with SSSJ leader Rabbi Avi Weiss and 28 other rabbis, chained themselves to the gates of the United Nations as part of a Soviet Jewry protest. The wife of one of his fellow protesters wrote to Rabbi Lookstein afterwards:

> Some wives are thrilled when their husbands give them a fur coat, a diamond bracelet, or a gold pin. Yesterday Sol gave me his Summons of Arrest and no gift in the world could have given me more pleasure. I'm very proud of Sol's participation in your demonstration, but you—you have given me a more precious gift. You've given me back my hope, my optimism for the future....[56]

The Ramaz students, who ranged in age from seventh graders [including Joshua Lookstein] to seniors, were apprehensive yet remained "serious and sober," as Rabbi Lookstein put it. "They refrained from improper behavior in front of the cameras. They were really outstanding." All 67 detainees were released after a short time without any charges being pressed. The television crew was waiting for them outside the station house and interviewed several of the students; Amanda Newman and Josh Rochlin "spoke movingly about why they felt it was important to participate in this protest."[57]

> The entire experience could only be described as a *Kiddush Ha-Shem*. Boys and girls of junior and senior high school age davened, chanted, and pleaded with God and with man for the safe-

ty and well-being of a heroic Jew 6,000 miles away. The entire demonstration was carried out with dignity and propriety. The students spoke intelligently and compassionately about their cause. ... It was good publicity for Sharansky; it was also an unforgettable experience of solidarity with a suffering Jew on the part of sixty-five young men and women who will never forget what they did and why they did it.

For Rabbi Lookstein too it was unforgettable, and in a more personal way. "I devoted four years of my life to writing a doctoral dissertation on the subject: 'What Were American Jews Doing While Six Million Died?'" he noted. "The answer to that question is 'not much.' ... [B]usiness went on pretty much as usual....There were no daily services outside on the street conducted by students or by adults.... Maybe Ramaz students have learned the lesson. Maybe they are even teaching us a lesson."

Rabbi Lookstein himself provided the students with the ideal role model for learning those lessons. The research for his dissertation had both sensitized him to American Jewry's disappointing record and energized him to ensure that past mistakes would not be repeated. One episode in particular epitomized the extent to which he had internalized the importance of that history. One autumn shortly before Yom Kippur he received a phone call from Zeesy Schnur at the Greater New York Conference on Soviet Jewry, asking him to attend a Jewish leadership summit for Soviet Jewry that would take place in Washington three days before the Day of Atonement. R. Haskel explained that his numerous High Holiday duties made his attendance impossible. "But as soon as I hung up the phone, I remembered how in 1943, three days before Yom Kippur, 400 rabbis left their pulpits and communities and came to Washington to plead for the rescue of Europe's Jews," he said. "It was no doubt a huge inconvenience for them, but they did it anyway. I had written about that episode in my book, and about how tragic it was that it was the only rally in Washington during the Holocaust. How could I do any less?" The rabbi immediately called Schnur back and said he would attend. But as fate would have it, just hours before the summit the Looksteins' daughter Mindy gave birth to their first grandchild, Michael Joseph. R. Haskel planned to cancel his trip to be with Mindy, but she insisted he go. Reluctantly he did so, on condition that when the boy was old enough, she would explain to him that the reason his grandfather could not be with them on the day he was born was that he had to go to Washington to help Soviet Jewry.[58]

R. Haskel had no regrets about the high level of involvement by his students in such activity, even at the expense of school time. "I always say, 'You should never allow school to interfere with your education.' Some people may think that's downgrading education, but I feel that it's actually upgrading education. Students can get more in an hour at an important demonstration than they can in three hours in class. The fact that our students wanted to do it was, in my mind, a tremendous triumph, because in the end that's what the shul and the school are all about—raising a generation that really cares." He never received any complaints from parents about their children missing classes, or even about the arrests, although after his own first arrest for Soviet Jewry his father expressed dismay that R. Haskel would have a police record. "He warned me that I would be barred for life from ever becoming president of the United States because of my record of arrests. It was a deprivation to which I submitted with great fortitude."[59]

In the wake of the mass arrest, the police agreed to permit the students to hold their morning minyan further down the block. So they continued to come day after day, prompting the Soviet Mission to formally complain to the United Nations that "Zionist hooligans are assembling daily in the vicinity of the Mission." Autumn turned to winter and temperatures plummeted, yet 40 to 60 students still came every frigid morning. Finally, on December 13, nearly two months after they began, with the temperature at just 18 degrees and the wind chill factor below zero, the students reluctantly heeded their rabbi's plea to end the vigil. There was, however, an important postscript to the vigil of 1982: in 2006 Ramaz students began davening *shacharit* in front of the Iranian Mission to the United Nations every Wednesday to protest Iran's Holocaust denial and its support for terrorist groups. Rabbi Lookstein's grandson David was one of the organizers and is a regular participant. The practice has continued through today.

After so many years of prayers and protests, hunger strikes and sit-downs, bulletin board reminders and marches down Fifth Avenue, one day in February 1986 it happened: Natan Sharansky was released from prison and flown out of the Soviet Union. Frustrated by the constant clamor of Soviet Jewry protesters in the United States and their ability to push the Sharansky issue onto the agenda of Soviet–American relations, the Kremlin finally decided that keeping Sharansky was more of a headache than letting him go. Rabbi Lookstein and the KJ-Ramaz community could justly feel proud of the important role they played in keeping Sharansky in the spotlight and galvanizing the American Jewish community to greater activism. The day before Sharansky's release, R. Haskel heard a brief, vague rumor about the possibility that something might happen, but when the news came over the radio it hit him "like a thunderclap." The Looksteins immediately booked a flight to Israel, even though they were scheduled to go again in just three weeks on a UJA Rabbinic Cabinet mission. "We had always promised ourselves that when he got out, we would drop everything to go see him. And we did."[60]

"The feeling of meeting him, in Jerusalem, after all those years of struggle, was indescribable," R. Haskel said. "It was nothing short of a miracle." After a long embrace, they sat down and Rabbi Lookstein presented Sharansky with a copy of *Were We Our Brothers' Keepers?* The dedication page read: "To Anatoly Scharansky<Au" Is this how it's spelled on the dedication page?>, a dear friend and a heroic Jew. You taught us the meaning of the Biblical command: 'Do not stand idly by while your brother's blood is spilled.' [Leviticus 19:16] One day soon we will present to you in Jerusalem a copy of this book, which you inspired." That day had finally arrived. "It stunned me to realize that only eight months after I wrote those words, it actually came to pass. I had never believed it would happen so quickly," he said. "What was also amazing is that when I handed him the book, Natan said, 'Oh, this was going to be your dissertation.' Even though I am sure I had only mentioned my dissertation topic in passing, he still remembered it, more than eleven years later, and despite everything he had endured during that time."[61]

Two months later Sharansky came to New York City to take part in Solidarity Sunday. Naturally his stop included a visit to Kehilath Jeshurun. The entire student body of Ramaz, nearly 1,000 children, packed the shul. Sharansky sat alongside the ark, in the chair that had held his poster every Rosh Hashana and Yom Kippur. [Photographs of Israeli MIAs now occupy that seat.] R. Haskel invited every student whose parents had gone as emissaries to the USSR to sit directly in front of Sharansky, on the steps leading up to the ark, as a gesture of thanks for their parents' involvement. More than 70 children came forward, vivid testimony to the high level of involvement by Ramaz parents in the Soviet Jewry movement. In his remarks, Sharansky expressed his appreciation to Rabbi Lookstein, Noam Shudofsky, the students of Ramaz, and the KJ membership for all their efforts over the years. He said he was particularly moved to learn of such gestures as the bulletin board in front of the synagogue, the students' daily minyan outside the Soviet Mission, and "Sharansky Day" at Ramaz.[62]

When Rabbi Lookstein gave Sharansky his tallis and tefillin in 1975, he wondered if the young refusenik would ever make use of them or come closer to Judaism in any way. Nearly three decades later at the Kotel, he would by accident discover the answer to that question. KJ's Thanksgiving Week mission to Israel in 2002 coincided with Shabbat Hanukkah, and the group davened on Friday night at the Wall. Someone in the KJ group informed Rabbi Lookstein that Sharansky was there too. "I looked around and, although it was very crowded and neither of us is very tall, sure enough I spotted his telltale army fatigue hat," R. Haskel said. "He was davening with students from Yeshivat HaKotel. The two of us embraced. I could not get over the fact that this man, who when I first met him did not know a siddur from a Herman Wouk novel, was now davening fluently, saying *kaddish*—his mother had passed away earlier that year—and everything else. I thought to myself, this is the fulfillment of the extra prayer that we were saying on Hanukkah—'for the miracles and the wonders that You did for our forefathers, in those days, at this time'— only, I thought 'in those days *and* in this time,' because it really was a wondrous sight."[63]

During the final years of the Soviet Jewry struggle, Rabbi Lookstein occasionally found himself at odds with individuals from the Orthodox community who favored a softer approach toward the Soviets. For example, a letter from New York City Councilman Noach Dear to the *New York Times,* minimizing the extent of anti-Semitism in the USSR, compelled R. Haskel to respond with both a letter to the *Times* and a more strongly worded private letter. "I was appalled by your readiness to judge the extent of anti-Semitism in the Soviet Union from the relative safety of an office or home here in New York," he wrote to Dear. "Is it fair to sit in New York and decide whether Soviet Jews are right or wrong about the threats being real or not? We had no right to do that fifty years ago, and we have no right to do it today."[64]

On another occasion Adolph Shayevitz, chief rabbi of Moscow, a strong critic of Zionism and the Soviet Jewry protest movement, was brought to the United States by Rabbis Arthur and Marc Schneier for a series of talks in which he essentially defended the Soviet regime. Rabbi Lookstein and his colleagues at the New York Board of Rabbis agreed to meet him so long as it would be strictly in private, "so that there should be no publicity whatsoever about the meeting which might hurt the cause of our brothers and sisters in the Soviet Union." R. Haskel and other officers of the Board of Rabbis presented Rabbi Shayevitz with an array of skeptical questions. Rabbi Lookstein, hoping the meeting could produce something positive rather than be a confrontation, expressed sympathy for "how hard it is for a rabbi with any congregation [and] how much harder it must be when the congregation includes the government officials of the Soviet Union." He then gave Rabbi Shayevitz a small pocket Tanach and asked him to deliver it to the imprisoned Natan Sharansky.[65]

The Looksteins' third visit to the USSR took place in May 1987, when they were sent by the Rabbinical Council of America [RCA] as part of a delegation. This was a period of growing turmoil within the Soviet Union. In response both to its own domestic problems and to the international economic and political pressure over human rights issues—of which the Soviet Jewry campaign was an important component—Soviet Premier Mikhail Gorbachev had begun instituting a series of reforms known as perestroika and glasnost, which involved loosening restrictions on freedom of speech, releasing political prisoners, and other significant changes. In response to these reforms, a delegation from the World Jewish Congress undertook what turned out to be a highly controversial visit to the USSR in early 1987, just prior to the RCA mission. To the chagrin of Soviet Jewish refuseniks, the WJC delegation offered to push for a waiver of the Jackson-Vanik Amendment's restrictions on trade with the USSR in exchange for alleged promises by Soviet officials to improve conditions for Russian Jews. After their visit, the WJC representatives suggested that the emigration issue should take a back seat to other concerns such as improving Jewish cultural life in the USSR.[66]

R. Haskel and the RCA delegation became engulfed in related turmoil when one member, Rabbi David Hollander, who preferred quiet diplomacy to public demonstrations, excluded Rabbi Lookstein from meetings with Soviet officials. Rabbi Hollander claimed to have secured Soviet assurances on such issues as opening a kosher restaurant in Moscow and permitting American rabbinical students to study in the USSR and Russian Jewish students to study at an American yeshiva. Rabbi Hollander and his organization, the Union of Orthodox Rabbis [Iggud Harabonim], subsequently urged a boycott of that year's mass rally for Soviet Jewry in Washington and met with Soviet diplomats in the United States to continue discussing issues unrelated to emigration.[67]

In private correspondence, Rabbi Lookstein characterized Rabbi Hollander's actions as "acts of travesty and stupidity" that would "lull people into an absolutely groundless sense of security." Sending "a few hand-picked lackeys" to study in the United States should not be presented as evidence of glasnost, he wrote. "That is wonderful for Gorbachev. He couldn't ask for better propaganda. But such statements could be a crushing blow to Soviet Jewish refuseniks" by undermining the chances of them receiving exit visas.[68] His public response to the Hollander group came in the form of an op-ed article entitled "Soviet Jewish Refusneniks Want Exit Visas Even More Than They Want Rabbis." The possibility of opening a kosher restaurant or sending rabbinical students to the Soviet Union "are interesting prospects but they should not distract us from the main goal of the refuseniks," he wrote. "That goal is emigration. It is their first, second, and third priorities. ... Jewish cultural and religious life in Russia is desirable— but emigration is critical."[69]

In a second op-ed piece later that year, urging Jews to attend the rally in Washington, Rabbi Lookstein said that a kosher restaurant in Moscow would "do a lot for Gorbachev and 'Rabbi' Shayevitz but very little for Soviet Jews. What is needed is one thing: free emigration."[70] Returning to a theme that appeared often in his writings and speeches about Soviet Jewry over the years, R. Haskel argued in the op-ed article that an important reason for attending the December 1987 demonstration was the memory of American Jewry's "indifference to Jewish suffering during World War II." The response of American Jews to news of the Holocaust "was pitifully weak. There were no rallies in Washington in December of 1942," despite the confirmation of the Nazi genocide that month. In a letter to the *Jewish Week* in response to a rabbi's denunciation of the rally, Rabbi Lookstein argued that advocates of that position "sound like the scared Jews of the 1930s and 1940s who said that we should not make loud noises for fear of endangering German Jewry and Polish Jewry. ... History has shown us that this view was wrong 45 and 50 years ago [and] it is still wrong today," as proven by the fact that the Soviets had permitted nearly 300,000 Jews to leave in the past fifteen years in response to world pressure. American Jews answered the call in 1987: in the largest rally in U.S. Jewish history, an estimated 250,000 protesters gathered in Washington, D.C., that December.[71]

While Rabbi Hollander urged an emphasis on religious and cultural assistance instead of emigration, Rabbi Lookstein advocated action on both fronts. In addition to his public activism for emigration, R. Haskel urged fellow rabbis to visit the USSR to provide Soviet Jews with religious aid. One of his earliest acts after becoming president of the New York Board of Rabbis in 1977 was to send a letter to all of its members, urging them to visit the Jews in the Soviet Union. Likewise after becoming chairman of the Yeshiva University Rabbinic Alumni Association in 1978, he used his position to press his fellow rabbis to go to Russia, even announcing that he would personally assist Y.U. graduates who were willing to go.[72] After becoming chairman of the RCA's Soviet Jewry Committee, he strongly encouraged RCA member-rabbis to visit the USSR, he raised funds to purchase tefillin and other religious articles to be smuggled into the Soviet Union, and he pressed rabbis to urge bar and bat mitzvah children to contribute part of their gift money to sponsor publication of small boxed sets of Russian-language *Chumashim* to be smuggled into the USSR.[73] The issue was a question of priorities. Between those who, at one extreme, were interested only in emigration, and those at the other extreme, such as Hollander, who wanted to focus solely on cultural matters, Rabbi Lookstein sought a golden mean: continuing demonstrations and other efforts to pressure the Soviets on emigration while simultaneously providing religious and educational assistance to Soviet Jews.

His 1987 visit behind the Iron Curtain reconfirmed for Rabbi Lookstein the wisdom of his dual approach. From the moment he and Audrey arrived and saw the customs officials barely check any of their luggage, they realized that, as he put it, "Yes, there is glasnost today in Russia and you can feel it." On their previous trips, "We felt as if we were in a prison. This time we did not have that feeling. We knew we were in a prison but it didn't feel like it."[74] One glance at downtown Moscow in 1987 told Audrey that things were changing. "On our previous visits, everything seemed gray and brown and depressed," she recalled. "But the first thing we noticed this time was how people were wearing brighter clothing, display windows in stores were colorful; it gave us the feeling that Russian society was starting to come alive again."[75]

Among the refuseniks, they found a strong conviction that with the advent of perestroika, a crucial window of opportunity had opened, and swift pressure on the Kremlin was needed by American Jewry and the U.S. government to ensure that Prisoners of Zion were released and exit visas increased significantly. "Unlike during the Holocaust," Rabbi Lookstein wrote in his report to the RCA,

> we cannot use what Hayim Greenberg called "an ox-cart express" while our foes keep the machinery of oppression humming. We have to work quickly and not waste a minute. I kept thinking of the Talmudic principle that a "mitzvah which comes to your hands should not be allowed to go sour." It must be done on the moment.[76]

Rabbi Lookstein urged his RCA colleagues to "listen to the refuseniks" in determining how to respond to glasnost. "They are there. They have the facts on the ground.... It's their life, not ours." The refuseniks feel that "culture and religion ought to be priorities, but not at the top of the list. The first, second, third, fourth, and fifth priorities are: emigration, emigration, and particularly emigration for long-term refuseniks.... A kosher restaurant in Moscow is not going to solve any problems.... We cannot transform Russia, they say, but Russia can manipulate us into pushing for something else other than emigration."[77]

One of the items in the rabbi's hand luggage that the customs officials never spotted was a videotape of a Solidarity Sunday rally, something that refuseniks in the Soviet Union had never seen. "Both of us were scared stiff, knowing that this was sitting in my carry-on bag," Rabbi Lookstein wrote to a colleague. "For the life of us, we couldn't figure out what we would say if the customs officials took it out and began to look at it." But they did not, and the next day the rabbi and Audrey sat with a group of refuseniks as they watched it. "To see them riveted on that tape for two hours, watching every nuance, taking in every word, was an incredible experience for us," R. Haskel recalled. "To see the excitement in Masha [Slepak] when she saw her children and grandchildren [who took part in the rally] was extremely moving."[78]

The meetings the Looksteins held during their week in Russia in 1987 illustrated how much the atmosphere had changed since their last visit twelve years earlier. One group of refuseniks, for example, described plans to begin publishing their previously banned magazine, *Jews in the USSR*, in view of the Kremlin's abolition of censorship. The Looksteins heard complaints about visiting rabbis—not that there were so few, as in 1975, but that while there were many who were visiting Jewish communities in large cities, they were needed in smaller cities as well. Conversations about kosher chickens, Passover matzahs, and Jewish books that were needed focused on the number needed for particular locales rather than the idea of any being available anywhere. Most remarkable was the fact that there was now a sufficient number of religiously observant refuseniks that there were three factions, each with its own particular approach to political, religious, and emigration issues. At a gathering in celebration of Yudi Edelstein's release from prison, the Looksteins marveled at the fact that Yuli, Eliyahu Essas, and a group of about twenty *ba'alei teshuva* washed with *mayim acharonim*, sang *Shir HaMaalot* to the tune of *Hatikva*, and then "bensched in a most fervent and pious manner. It was something which we never anticipated seeing in the Soviet Union after our visits in '72 and '75."[79]

One morning near the end of their stay in the USSR, while davening at the Moscow synagogue, Rabbi Lookstein was asked to serve as the Torah reader. "I agreed to despite the fact that I wasn't sure I knew the particular *parsha* well enough. Somebody upstairs—the same One who always guides us around when we are in the Soviet Union—improved my memory and I managed to do very well." R. Haskel then made a *misheberach* for a new baby girl, born to the wife of Alexander Kholmiansky, "and we followed the *misheberach* by singing together with everybody *Siman Tov U'Mazel Tov*. It was just as if we were in KJ here in New York."[80]

On their last day, after a meal with a group of refuseniks, Rabbi Lookstein led the grace after meals. As he did so and glanced around the table, he realized that everyone there had been waiting more than fifteen years to leave the USSR. "As I came to the end of the *bensching* I began to sing *HaShem Oz L'Amo Yitein,* may God give his people strength and may God bless his people with peace, and without realizing it, both Audrey and I suddenly became choked up," he recalled. "Later on we both realized that we were thinking of the same thing. God has given our people in the Soviet Union an incredible amount of strength. But it is high time that He gave them some peace as well." With continued activism, he was convinced, "Peace will come to all of our friends at this critical hour, a moment in history which none of us dare waste."[81]

The RCA leadership endorsed Rabbi Lookstein's perspective. In effect rebuffing Rabbi Hollander's efforts, the RCA distributed a letter to its constituents urging them to attend the Washington rally, warning that despite glasnost, "the overall picture for Soviet Jews remains extremely bleak," and urging the American Jewish community to "continue to apply pressure and express our indignation and protest until there is a true liberalization of emigration policy and the opportunity for a fuller Jewish life inside the Soviet Union." In a letter to Rabbi Lookstein, RCA president Rabbi Milton Polin described as a "canard" Rabbi Hollander's claim that the leading Torah authorities opposed demonstrations [on the grounds that rallies might provoke a backlash by the Kremlin against Soviet Jewry].[82] The RCA also resolved to continue urging its members to take part in missions to the Soviet Union, as Rabbi Lookstein recommended.

Rabbis were not the only ones whom R. Haskel urged to visit the USSR. After returning from his mission in 1972, he initiated a program, administered by Noam Shudofsky, to send KJ members to the Soviet Union. Over the course of fifteen years, more than 50 KJ or Ramaz alumni couples went. Ramaz students went too, on a series of separate missions. Although accompanied by faculty members, the missions still meant sending young teenagers into a distant and hostile country, although by the time of the visits, in 1986 and 1988, conditions in the USSR had eased sufficiently to put most parents' fears to rest.

In early 1989 Rabbi Lookstein was named chairman of the Coalition to Free Soviet Jews [formerly the Greater New York Conference on Soviet Jewry]. With perestroika and glasnost in full swing, Prisoners of Zion were being set free and the rate of Soviet Jewish emigration skyrocketed. By the end of 1989 it would reach an all-time annual high of 70,000. With many refuseniks still denied exit visas and the overall situation so uncertain, the Coalition at first continued many of its previous activities, although Solidarity Sunday was canceled and it seemed inevitable that the organization would shift from demanding emigration to coping with the huge flow of emigrants.

When the Looksteins traveled to the USSR in December of that year, for their fourth and final mission, they saw firsthand the drastic changes that had taken place. Meetings with Jewish activists in Moscow focused on the need to send more emissaries "to bring these people closer to Judaism" in the last months before their seemingly imminent emigration. In Leningrad there were "probably more young people than old people" in the synagogue, a reversal of what the Looksteins experienced in their 1970s visits. More than 700 local Jews were studying Hebrew, and "700 more want to learn but cannot because there are not enough teachers." Preparations were underway to establish a day school. The Looksteins spent a number of days in a smaller city, Kharkov, which had been neglected by most emissaries to the USSR. At a Friday night gathering in the home of a local Hebrew teacher, the Looksteins spent five hours praying, teaching, singing, and guiding the participants through the first Shabbat observance that many of them had ever experienced. (The ritual handwashing and recitation of the appropriate blessings alone took thirty minutes, because none of them had ever done it before.)[83]

Despite the relatively small size of the Kharkov Jewish community, there were 500 Jews studying Hebrew, and another 300 on a waiting list. The Looksteins met with local activists, assessed their specific needs, and even filed a complaint with the local authorities about careless damage done to the synagogue's water pipes, prompting assurances that the Jewish community would receive better protection. ("What a difference a couple of years can make!" R. Haskel wrote in his report.) As on their previous trips, Rabbi Lookstein spent considerable time showing local activists the basics of Jewish practice: *kiddush*, *ha-motzi*, Shabbat songs, prayers, *birkat ha-mazon*, and the like. He even managed to perform a wedding before the trip ended.[84]

In a post-trip report co-authored with traveling companions Zeesy Schnur and Ezra Levin of the Coalition to Free Soviet Jews, Rabbi Lookstein grappled with the question of whether the Coalition should continue to exist. Their conclusion was that it was too soon to go out of business. Although there had been many months of large-scale immigration, they could not yet be certain the trend would continue, and it would be too difficult later to rebuild a disbanded organization. Moreover, even if emigration continued at a high rate, the Coalition was still needed to organize American rabbis and other emissaries to go to the USSR to assist in the "Judaization" of a community that had been forcibly assimilated for 70 years. "Jewishness and Judaism are exploding inside the Soviet Union," Rabbi Lookstein told a UJA-Federation meeting called to discuss whether to continue funding the Coalition. "Jews who would never have thought of emigrating to Israel are now doing so. A totally secular Soviet Jew sitting next to a cab driver on our drive in Kharkov told us that he has friends in Haifa and Tel Aviv and therefore he is going to Israel. This young man had as much a connection with Jewishness as I have with being an astronaut. ... You and I have a job to do—we have to fuel that resurgence of Judaism that is taking place and make sure that when Soviet Jews arrive in Israel they do not come raw but rather as well prepared as they possibly can be."[85]

Toward that end, the Coalition undertook a number of programs, including a live telephone hookup between Jews in six Soviet cities and a Ramaz Hanukkah assembly ("You have no idea how beautiful it was for us in Tashkent to hear Jewish children singing *Hatikva*," a Soviet Jewish woman in that Central Asian region told the interpreter), Torah lessons given by telephone to the USSR by Ramaz faculty and other rabbis, monthly missions to the USSR by Hebrew and Judaic Studies teachers, and expansion of bar mitzvah twinning projects and the sending of books and tapes.[86] With the final collapse of the Soviet Union in 1991 and the drastic expansion of services provided by other American Jewish organizations and the Israeli government, the Coalition for Soviet Jews found its activities supplanted by other agencies that were better equipped for such efforts. In 1993 the Coalition ceased its regular operations and became a commission of the Jewish Community Relations Council. Rabbi Lookstein's two decades of Soviet Jewry activism had reached their gratifying conclusion.

## NOTES

[1] "Talmud Is Called Civil Rights Guide," *New York Times*, 15 May 1966; RHL, "'And Proclaim Liberty Throughout the Land': A Biblical Prescription for 'The American Dilemma'" [sermon], undated [1966], File: Sermons, KJ.

[2] Haskel Lookstein, "A Word About 'Kosher' Lettuce," KJB XXXIX:11 [5 February 1971], p. 2; "Are California Table Grapes Kosher?" KJB LIV:4 [19 December 1986], p. 6.

[3] Glenn Richter interview with Rafael Medoff, 7 March 2008.

[4] The term 'separatist' is used here to refer to yeshivas whose philosophy is to keep as separate as possible from secular society, in contrast to Centrist, or Modern, Orthodoxy, which advocates participation in secular society while maintaining Orthodox religious observance. The term *haredi* is usually used in Israel to designate those adhering to a separatist philosophy, although that term has not yet become commonplace in the United States.

[5] "Another Capacity Audience Attends Men's Club Meeting," KJB XXXIII:11 [21 November 1964], p. 1; "Teenagers Discuss Russian Jewry," KJB XXXIII:16 [1 January 1965], p. 2; "Capacity Audience Hears Moving Report on Soviet Jewry by Rabbi Israel Miller," KJB XXXIV:8 [5 November 1965], p. 3; "That the Jews of the Soviet Union May Know That They Have Not Been Forgotten...," KJB XXXIV:27 [1 April 1966], p. 3; "Haskel Lookstein, "Noah and Selfishness," KJB XXXV:4 [14 October 1966], p. 2; "Special Service for Students as Part of Soviet Jewry Vigil Sunday, Chol ha-Moed, at U.N.," KJB XXXV:28 [21 April 1967], p. 5; "Our Youth Vigil for Soviet Jewry," KJB XXXV:29 [12 May 1967], p. 4; "Petition on Behalf of

Silent Soviet Jewry," KJB XXXVII:11 [6 December 1968], p. 5; "One Thousand Signatures Sent to United Nations in Behalf of Russian Jewry," KJB XXXVII:13 [27 December 1968], p. 1.

[6] Haskel Lookstein to the Editor of the *New York Times*, 4 February 1969, File: *New York Times*, KJ; "Kehilath Jeshurun Host to 20,000 at Mass Prayer and Protest Meeting for Iraqi Jewry," KJB XXXVII:18 [7 February 1969], p. 1.

[7] George Palmer, Assistant to the Managing Editor, to Haskel Lookstein, 19 February 1969, File: *New York Times*, KJ.

[8] "Purim Notes for Parents and Children," KJB XXXIX:13 [5 March 1971], p. 1; "Over 1,000 Attend Babi Yar Memorial at K.J.," KJB XL:3 [8 October 1971], p. 3; "KJSJ Daveners at the Isaiah Wall with Dr. Mikhail Zand," KJB XL:4 [22 October 1971], p. 5; Haskel Lookstein, "A Suggestion for Chanukah," KJB XL:5 [5 November 1971], p. 2; "Freedom Lights for Soviet Jewry," KJB XL:8 [17 December 1971], p. 1.

[9] To Rabbi Lookstein's apology for "speaking such a broken Yiddish," the man replied, "No, you speak beautiful Yiddish," prompting Rabbi Joseph Lookstein to later joke, "If you had been speaking Yiddish, he would have said it was beautiful." RHL interview, 16 August 2007.

[10] "Report on Visit of Rabbi and Mrs. Haskel Lookstein to the Soviet Union, September 19–October 2 [1972]," p. 2, File: Soviet Jewry, KJ

[11] Robert G. Kaiser, "Soviets Restrict Jewish Celebration," *Washington Post*, 2 October 1972.

[12] "Report on Visit of Rabbi and Mrs. Haskel Lookstein to the Soviet Union, September 19–October 2 [1972]," p. 3, File: Soviet Jewry, KJ.

[13] Alexander Luntz memoir in *Teacher, Preacher*, p.72.

[14] "Report on Visit of Rabbi and Mrs. Haskel Lookstein to the Soviet Union, September 19–October 2 [1972]," pp.3–4, File: Soviet Jewry, KJ.

[15] Ibid., p. 4.

[16] Ibid., pp. 5–6.

[17] Ibid., pp. 8–12.

[18] Ibid., p.14.

[19] RHL Interview, 16 August 2007.

[20] RHL to Members and Friends, 10 October 1972, File: Soviet Jewry, KJ.

[21] RHL to Stanley Lowell, 11 July 1972, File: Soviet Jewry, KJ.

[22] RHL interview, 25 July 2007.

[23] RHL Interview, 18 September 2007; Rabbi Baruch Silverstein and Rabbi Haskel Lookstein to Colleagues, 6 March 1979, File: Soviet Jewry, KJ.

[24] Rabbi Joseph Deitcher to Colleagues, 2 November 1982, File: Soviet Jewry, KJ.

[25] Yizkor—Remember: A Service of Prayer, Congregation Kehilath Jeshurun, pp. 14–15.

[26] RHL Interview, 18 September 2007; Jenna Weissman Joselit, *New York's Jewish Jews: The Orthodox Community in the Interwar Years* [Bloomington and Indianapolis: Indiana University Press, 1990], pp. 21,160 n.111.

[27] RHL interview, 18 September 2007.

[28] Rabbi Haskel Lookstein to Joshua Justman, 17 November 1975, File: Soviet Jewry, KJ.

[29] Rabbi Haskel Lookstein to various recipients, 8 March 1976, File: Soviet Jewry, KJ.

[30] Rabbi Haskel Lookstein, "Report on Visit of Rabbi and Mrs. Haskel Lookstein to the Soviet Union,September 16–October 2, 1975," File: Soviet Jewry, KJ, pp. 1–2.

[31] Ibid., p. 2.

[32] Audrey Lookstein interview.

[33] Rabbi Haskel Lookstein, "Report on Visit of Rabbi and Mrs. Haskel Lookstein to the Soviet Union,September 16–October 2, 1975," File: Soviet Jewry, KJ, pp. 2–3.

[34] Natan Sharansky memoir in *Teacher, Preacher* , p. 76.

[35] Ibid.

[36] RHL interview, 10 January 2008.

[37] Ibid.

[38] Ibid.

[39] Ibid.

[40] Rabbi Haskel Lookstein, "Report on Visit of Rabbi and Mrs. Haskel Lookstein to the Soviet Union,September 16–October 2, 1975," File: Soviet Jewry, KJ, p. 8; Rabbi Haskel Lookstein to Joshua Justman, 17 November 1975, File: Soviet Jewry, KJ., p. 2.

[41] RHL Interview, 8 January 2008.

[42] Rabbi Haskel Lookstein, "Report on Visit of Rabbi and Mrs. Haskel Lookstein to the Soviet Union,September 16–October 2, 1975," File: Soviet Jewry, KJ, p. 8; RHL interview, 10 January 2008.

[43] "A K.J.S.J. Report to Its Members and Friends," KJB, 19 January 1973, p.1; Noam Shudofsky to Fred Grubel, 12 May 1975, File: Soviet Jewry, KJ; Memo, "Telford Taylor Project," 4 March 1975, File: Soviet Jewry, KJ; Raphael Recananti to Rabbi Haskel Lookstein, 2 April 1976, File: Soviet Jewry, KJ; Robbie Bensley to Board Members of Kehilath Jeshurun for Soviet Jewry, 12 December 1975, File: Soviet Jewry, KJ; Mrs. Samuel Eisenstat and Harry Kleinhaus to Members of Kehilath Jeshurun for Soviet Jewry, 18 November 1974, File: Soviet Jewry, KJ; Harry Green and Gilbert Kahn, "Memorandum to the Community," 6 February 1973, File: Soviet Jewry, KJ.

[44] Rabbi Haskel Lookstein to Rabbis Judah Cahn, Louis Gerstein, Gunter Hirschberg, Edward Klein, and Ronald Sobel, 5 May 1976, File: Soviet Jewry, KJ.

[45] Rabbi Haskel Lookstein, "Solidarity Day 1980 Evaluation: Basis for Discussion" [undated], File: Soviet Jewry, KJ.

[46] Rabbi Haskel Lookstein memo to Solidarity Day '81 Committee, 23 September 1980, File: Soviet Jewry, KJ; "September 30, 1980 Solidarity Day '81 Committee Meeting—Summary of Discussion," File: Soviet Jewry,KJ.

[47] Rabbi Haskel Lookstein, Draft of Greater New York Conference letter to rabbis [undated], File: Soviet Jewry, KJ.

[48] Natan Sharansky memoir in *Teacher, Preacher* , p. 76.

[49] Danielle Lassner interview with Rafael Medoff, 27 November 2007; Mindy Cinnamon interview, op.cit

[50] RHL to yeshiva day school principals, 14 November 1972, File: Soviet Jewry, KJ.

[51] RHL to yeshiva day school principals, 30 November 1972, File: Soviet Jewry, KJ.

[52] "They Speak for Jews of Russia," *New York Daily News,* 4 February 1973, p. 47; Arlene Agus to Rabbi Haskel Lookstein, 28 January 1976, File: Soviet Jewry, KJ; Ramaz News Release, 8 June 1977, File: Soviet Jewry, KJ; Margy Ruth-Davis to Rabbi Haskel Lookstein, 15 October 1976, File: Soviet Jewry, KJ.

[53] Shira Baruch interview; RHL to Rabbi Noah Golinkin, 4 June 1986, File: Book, KJ.

[54] Rivka Rosenwein, "An Ex-Martyr on Parade," *Wall Street Journal,* 14 May 1986.

[55] Elenore Lester, "School Stages All-Day Fast-Protest to Tell Sharansky He's Not Alone," *Jewish Week-American Examiner,* 26 March 1978; "Natalia Scharansky, Wife of Imprisoned Soviet Refusnik, Addresses Ramaz School Student Body in Hunger Strike" [news release], 15 March 1978, File: Soviet Jewry, KJ.

[56] RHL, "Thoughts at a Chain-In," KJB XLIV:4 [12 November 1976], p. 3; Bertha Shoulson to RHL, 8 June 1977, File: Soviet Jewry, KJ.

[57] RHL interview, 18 September 2007; Rabbi Haskel Lookstein, "The Anatomy of a Protest" [New York: Ramaz School, 1983].

[58] RHL Interview , 18 September 2007; "Why We Are Here—Closing Statement of Rabbi Haskel Lookstein at the National Leadership Mission for Soviet Jewry in Washington at the Capitol Building, Wednesday, October 8, 1986," File: Soviet Jewry, KJ

[59] RHL, 18 September 2007; Rabbi Haskel Lookstein, "Acceptance Address Upon Election as Chairman of Coalition to Free Soviet Jews, Monday, January 23, 1989," File: Soviet Jewry, KJ, p. 4.

[60] Rabbi Haskel Lookstein, "We Remember Shcharansky," undated [May 1986], File: Soviet Jewry, KJ.

[61] RHL interview, 10 January 2008.

[62] A note from Elie Wiesel to Sharansky congratulating him on his freedom, urging him to accept Rabbi Lookstein's invitation to speak at Kehilath Jeshurun, noting, "No one has done more for you or for Soviet Jews. Ask Avital, she will confirm this."

[Elie Wiesel to Anatoly Sharansky, 9 February 1986, File: Soviet Jewry, KJ.]

[63] RHL interview, 8 January 2008.

[64] Rabbi Haskel Lookstein to Hon. Noach Dear, 26 March 1990, File: Soviet Jewry, KJ.

[65] Rabbi Haskel Lookstein, "A Private Encounter with the Rabbi of Moscow," 14 May 1984, File: Soviet Jewry, KJ.

[66] Audrey and Haskel Lookstein, "Moscow's Refuseniks Grapple with Glasnost: A Report on the Views of Soviet Jews, May 5–12, 1987," File: Soviet Jewry, KJ, pp. 3–4.; Henry L. Feingold, "Silent No More": Saving the Jews of Russia, The American Jewish Effort, 1967–1989 [Syracuse, N.Y.: Syracuse University Press, 2007], pp. 269–270.

[67] Rabbi Haskel Lookstein to Rabbi Binyamin Walfish and Rabbi Milton Polin, 10 June 1987, File: Soviet Jewry, KJ; Rabbi Milton Polin to Rabbi Haskel Lookstein, 16 June 1987, File: Soviet Jewry, KJ; Rabbi Binyamin Walfish to Rabbi Haskel Lookstein, 6 July 1987, File: Soviet Jewry, KJ; Rabbi Haskel Lookstein to Rabbi BInyamin Walfish, 15 July 1987, File: Soviet Jewry, KJ; Rabbi Haskel Lookstein to Dr. Oscar Z. Fasman, Rabbi Dr. Baruch A. Poupko, and Rabbi Solomon Roodman, 23 July 1987, File: Soviet Jewry, KJ; Rabbi Haskel Lookstein to Rabbi Baruch A. Poupko, 12 October 1987, File: Soviet Jewry, KJ; Rabbi Haskel Lookstein to Rabbi David Hollander, 12 October 1987, File: Soviet Jewry, KJ; Rabbi David Hollander to Rabbi Haskel Lookstein, 22 October 1987, File: Soviet Jewry, KJ.

[68] Rabbi Haskel Lookstein to Rabbi Judea B. Miller, 11 June 1987, File: Soviet Jewry, KJ; Rabbi Haskel Lookstein to Rabbi Binyamin Walfish and Rabbi Milton Polin, 10 June 1987, File: Soviet Jewry, KJ.

[69] Rabbi Haskel Lookstein, "Soviet Jewish Refuseniks Want Exit Visas Even More Than They Want Rabbis," undated [June 1987], KJ.

[70] Several months later, when no such restaurant had yet been opened, Rabbi Lookstein was unsettled by a reference to it in a letter from students' Soviet Jewry group. "No kosher restaurant has been opened," he wrote to the students. "It is the figment of the imagination and public relations of the Soviet Union and one particular American rabbi who feeds off that kind of misleading information." [Rabbi Haskel Lookstein to Student Coalition for Soviet Jewry, 29 February 1988, File: Soviet Jewry, KJ.]

[71] Rabbi Haskel Lookstein, "Why I Must Attend Soviet Jewry Rally," *New York Jewish Week*, 4 December 1987; Unpublished letter to the *New York Jewish Week*, 22 December 1987, File: Soviet Jewry, KJ.

[72] Rabbi Haskel Lookstein to Members of the New York Board of Rabbis, 10 March 1977, File: Soviet Jewry, KJ; Minutes of Executive Committee, Yeshiva University Rabbinic Alumni, 13 December 1978, File: Soviet Jewry, KJ.

[73] Rabbi Haskel Lookstein letter to RCA colleagues, August 1988, File: Soviet Jewry,

KJ; Rabbi Haskel Lookstein letter to RCA colleagues, 6 October 1986, File: Soviet Jewry, KJ.

[74] Audrey and Haskel Lookstein, "Moscow's Refuseniks Grapple," p.1.

[75] Audrey Lookstein interview.

[76] Audrey and Haskel Lookstein, "Moscow's Refuseniks Grapple." Greenberg, editor of the U.S. Labor Zionist journal *Jewish Frontier*, wrote in a 1943 critique of American Jewry's response to the slaughter of European Jewry: "[A]t a time when the Angel of Death uses airplanes, the A[merican]J[ewish]Congress employs an oxcart-express." [The text of Greenberg's article was reprinted in Shlomo Katz, "6,000,000 and 5,000,000 [Notes in Midstream]," *Midstream* X:1 [March 1964], pp. 3–14.

[77] Ibid., p.4.

[78] Rabbi Haskel Lookstein to Zeesy Schnur, 13 May 1987, File: Soviet Jewry, KJ.

[79] Audrey and Haskel Lookstein, "Moscow's Refuseniks Grapple," p. 9.

[80] Ibid., p.12.

[81] Ibid., p.13.

[82] Rabbi Milton Polin to Rabbi Haskel Lookstein, 14 January 1988, File: Soviet Jewry, KJ. Rabbi Polin included clippings from the Hebrew and Yiddish press citing prominent rabbinical authorities who endorsed demonstrations. The clippings had been sent to him by Rabbi Aaron Shurin, who, interestingly enough, was one of the 500 rabbis who took part in the only rally in Washington during the Holocaust, a rally cited by Rabbi Lookstein in his book, and in many speeches, as a source of personal inspiration to him.

[83] Haskel Lookstein, "The Jewish Heart Beats in the Soviet Union," *New York Jewish Week*, 23 February 1990.

[84] Rabbi Haskel Lookstein, "Mission to the Soviet Union: December 2, 1989–January 3, 1990," File: Soviet Jewry, KJ.

[85] Rabbi Haskel Lookstein, Ezra Levin, and Zeesy Schnur, "Why the Coalition for Soviet Jews in New York Must Continue Its Work," 15 January 1990, File: Soviet Jewry, KJ; "Rabbi Haskell [sic] Lookstein Remarks, Combined Meeting, January 22, 1990," File: Soviet Jewry, KJ.

[86] D. J. Saunders, "Shalom to Soviet Jews," *New York Daily News*, 20 October 1989; Haskel Lookstein, "New Realities Demand New Reactions," undated, File: Soviet Jewry, KJ; RHL, "Principal's Letter," 13 December 1989, File: Ramaz, KJ, p .4

# VII. WOMEN'S ISSUES

The original by-laws of Kehilath Jeshurun, which were typical of American Orthodox synagogues established in the nineteenth century or the first half of the twentieth, did not consider women to be individual members of the synagogue and did not grant them the right to vote at the annual meeting. A married couple was considered one member, and a single woman was merely an associate member. In practice, KJ's annual vote was conducted by a show of hands, and no vote was ever seriously contested, so when women, erroneously assuming they had the right to vote, raised their hands along with everyone else, nobody objected. But the principle of inequality remained in place, as did the reality that if they were not members, they could not serve as trustees or officers either. Thus they were legally unable to assume any leadership position in the synagogue. This imbalance would not sit well with Rabbi Lookstein indefinitely.

As a product of the Ramaz system, with its co-educational classes in all subjects from elementary through high school, R. Haskel entered the rabbinate with a sympathy for women's concerns that was atypical of American Orthodox rabbis. His inclination was tempered, however, by the public atmosphere of the late 1950s and early 1960s, in which women were consigned to a subordinate role at home, in the workplace, and in their houses of worship. Among American Orthodox women, such as those who belonged to KJ, there was relatively little sentiment for significant religious or social change. But amidst the rise of feminism and the women's liberation movement in the 1960s and early 1970s, an increasing number of Orthodox women began raising questions about their status in communal and religious life.

In early 1971 R. Haskel declared, in a sermon, that the time had come for Orthodox synagogues, including KJ, to permit women not only to be full individual members but also to serve on their boards. At the next meeting of the KJ board, Max Etra, who had recently retired after nearly three decades as president, upbraided the rabbi for his statements. "Mr. Etra felt that this was a form of propaganda and that it did not belong in the pulpit," the minutes reported. The criticism indicated the persistence among a segment of the KJ community and leadership of old-world attitudes about women's roles.[1]

The gradually simmering debate at KJ over women's concerns emerged full blown in June 1974, when women formally asked the Special Projects Committee for a change in the conduct of the Simchat Torah celebrations. Until then, women had been sitting in the balcony, essentially as spectators, while the men danced with the Torah scrolls below. Jean Blumenthal informed the committee that "all women to whom she had spoken want to be downstairs," in an area separated by a *mechitza*. The minutes recorded: "The time had come, said Jean, when the wishes of the women could no longer be ignored." Several men objected that having the women downstairs would unfairly reduce the area in which men and children could dance. Despite their objections, a resolution allowing women downstairs, with "overflow men" directed to the balconies, was approved by a vote of 12 to 2.[2] In addition, a Simchat Torah Committee was appointed to consider the matter. It subsequently reported to Rabbi Lookstein its view that despite the danger of overcrowding, it was "crucial that female congregants play a much more active role during the services and not be relegated to an observer status upstairs."[3]

But the issue was not yet concluded. At the next meeting of the Special Projects Committee, it was reported that all but one of the officers opposed having women sit downstairs. They claimed that "only a limited number of women" actually wanted to sit there, that the use of the *mechitza* would "severely hamper" the dancing, and that older members would object to having to sit in the balcony. After a vigorous debate, a motion was made to proceed with having an area for women downstairs. It passed, albeit narrowly: six in favor, five against, and one abstention.[4]

The following year Rabbi Lookstein proposed that the Yeshiva University rabbinic alumni devote their entire annual conference to issues such as women's prayer services, women serving as trustees or officers of their synagogues, and the problem of agunot, women whose ex-husbands would not grant them a religious divorce [a "*get*"]. The time had come, he urged his colleagues, for a full discussion of "Orthodoxy's response to a basic change in society's attitude toward women and in women's attitude toward themselves." Looking for practical solutions rather than just theoretical discussions, Rabbi Lookstein urged that the conference emphasize "making concrete halakhic and programmatic proposals to deal with these issues. We could then take these proposals to the highest rabbinic authorities and try to get specific approval or action upon them." The conference, however, did not materialize.[5]

In 1976 R. Haskel decided the time had come to confront the issue of women serving as members or officers of his synagogue. He asked Rabbi Soloveitchik for a specific ruling on the subject and was told that women could be members. In addition, the Rav ruled that women could also serve as trustees, since trustees deal with corporate issues and women have the same responsibilities as men in those areas. Rabbi Soloveitchik was undecided, however, on the question of women serving as officers, such as president or vice president. Those positions were related to the halakhic issue of a king's authority, and in Jewish tradition there is no concept of being ruled by a queen, only a king. As a result, the amended by-laws drafted in 1976 by R. Haskel, together with KJ members Irwin Robbins and Martin Markson, enabled women to serve as both members and trustees but also included this proviso: "By virtue of a halakhic opinion of Rabbi Joseph B.

Soloveitchik, women shall not be eligible to be officers of the congregation."[6]

A handful of older members at KJ felt uncomfortable about women becoming members or trustees, regarding such changes as an expression of feminism that was too radical for traditional Jewish life. But Rabbi Lookstein's presentation of the Rav's *psak* [religious ruling] to the board of trustees put the issue to rest and the new by-laws were adopted without incident on May 6, 1976. Ami Texon, a daughter of Rabbi Henry Raphael Gold and president of the KJ sisterhood, was immediately made the first woman trustee.[7]

In the months that followed, there was ample evidence of the changing attitudes within the congregation. The KJ newsletter began publishing bat mitzvah notices, complete with photos of the bat mitzvah girls, just as it had always done for bar mitzvah boys. The first *simchat bat* ceremony for a new baby girl was held at KJ that fall. At the next year's Simchat Torah festivities, "The Hakafot [dancing with the Torah scrolls] were never like this before," the newsletter reported. "Round and round the shul we danced—and the women too, for the first time; and they outlasted the men in both song and dance." By 1979 the appeal for attendance at the Father and Son Minyan was titled "Calling Fathers [and Mothers] and Sons [and Daughters]."[8]

R. Haskel's efforts regarding women members reflected several important aspects of his personal outlook and agenda. First, that wherever possible, without transgressing halakha, Orthodox practice should be brought into line with modern sensibilities. Second, that every effort should made to make Orthodoxy as attractive as possible both to its adherents and to the non-Orthodox. Third, that Orthodoxy should be as tolerant and inclusive as possible.

A dispute in Israel in 1986 brought these issues to the fore. Mrs. Leah Shakdiel, an Orthodox woman, was appointed by the municipality of her small home town, Yeroham, to serve on the local religious council, a government-funded body that administers synagogues and mikvas. Until Shakdiel's selection, the religious councils had been the exclusive province of men. The Religious Affairs Ministry and the chief rabbinate sought to block Mrs. Shakdiel's appointment. Rabbi Lookstein regarded the position of the Israeli rabbinical establishment as a minefield. "The establishment has backed itself into a corner" by taking the position that women cannot serve on such councils "and is engaged in a struggle which cannot be won without very serious losses," he wrote. One of those losses would be the damage to the public image of Orthodox Judaism, which would be seen as anti-woman. In addition, keeping Mrs. Shakdiel off the council might have the effect of alienating young Orthodox women from traditional Judaism. In the hope of contributing to a resolution of the conflict, Rabbi Lookstein decided to violate his own self-imposed policy of not publicly commenting on Israeli internal affairs. "I happen to be among those who believe that American Jews should not meddle in the internal affairs of Israel," he explained to a newspaper editor. "If you really want to affect Israeli policy, you have to make the leap of aliyah and do it from Israel." In this case, however, he believed that a public statement by himself and other American rabbis might help "create an atmosphere in which the religious establishment could retreat from a position which is so detrimental to religious life in Israel."[9]

"Without wishing to interfere in the matter," he wrote in a letter to a number of his rabbinical colleagues, it was necessary to show Israel's religious establishment "that we have fought this battle in America and resolved the problem without any losses whatsoever. Perhaps the example of how the problem has been resolved here will be of some help in resolving it in Israel." He asked them to co-sign a statement of protest, and nineteen of the rabbis he contacted agreed to do so.[10]

The statement they issued argued that while in ritual matters there were halakhic strictures governing women's roles, "in corporate matters [in a synagogue or a religious council], there is a great deal that can be done and has been done to assure that all members of the community—men and women—have the same voice in the corporate affairs of the community.... In America, most Orthodox congregations recognize the equal responsibility of men and women in the administrative functions of the synagogue."

Rabbi Lookstein and his colleagues also pointed out that "almost all Orthodox congregations have equal status for men and women as members; many have women on their board of trustees; and a number have women as officers."[11] KJ, however, was not yet one of the latter. That situation would change in 1999, six years after the Rav's passing, when Rabbi Lookstein decided to revisit the issue after reviewing a *shiur* by Rav Hershel Schachter explaining that Rav Soloveitchik's concerns about women serving as officers did not apply to the actual duties of an officer at KJ.[12] On that basis, KJ's by-laws were changed to permit women to serve as officers. The first woman president of a major Orthodox synagogue was appointed in 1997 (in Englewood, N.J.), and although the phenomenon of women presidents at Orthodox synagogues remains uncommon, there is little doubt that a woman could serve as president of KJ without opposition.

The issue of women's tefillah [prayer] groups arose relatively late at KJ. What was apparently the first women's tefillah group in the U.S. Orthodox community was organized at Lincoln Square Synagogue on Manhattan's Upper West Side in 1972. Similar groups were created at other Orthodox synagogues throughout the 1970s and 1980s. Interest in forming such a group at KJ emerged only in the late 1980s. It came from women who had been active in areas of synagogue life in which women typically played a prominent role, such as the *chevra kaddisha*, *bikur cholim* [visiting the sick], and adult education. Now they sought to have more personal involvement in such ritual aspects of synagogue life as prayer and Torah reading. In accordance with his general approach of tolerance and inclusiveness, Rabbi Lookstein regarded such groups sympathetically. In his view, "Women should be given every opportunity to express their religious commitment and to be as involved as possible in ritual, as long as it is done within an absolute halakhic framework. Whatever halakha will allow for women, should be done."[13]

There were murmurings of opposition within KJ from those who feared that a separate women's tefillah group, and particularly the prospect of women reading from the Torah at such groups, represented too much of a break from customary practices. R. Haskel checked with a colleague who had once discussed with Rabbi Soloveitchik the permissibility of a women's tefillah group at Brandeis University. He told Rabbi Lookstein that "the Rav did not say he was in favor of such a group, but instead said, 'If they're going to do it, here's the way they should do it,'" which included leaving out of their tefillah all parts of the regular service that require a minyan, and reading from the Torah without the usual blessings.

On that basis, R. Haskel devoted his Shabbat HaGadol sermon in 1988 to the question of such tefillah groups. The women who participated in the groups were not "a bunch of fanatic feminists looking for their place in the religious sun," he told his congregants. Nor were they "looking for kicks or fights—just for a personal experience in prayer which they cannot find in the balcony.... There are new needs which Jewish women have today to participate personally in tefillah as they do in life." Actually, those needs were not entirely new—as he noted in a later sermon, Miriam and the other Jewish women who sang at the Red Sea constituted "the first women's tefillah group."[14]

Some limitations were necessary, he ruled: the group's tefillot needed to be limited to those sections of the liturgy that did not require a minyan; there could be no separate women's reading of *Megillat Esther* on Purim, an event R. Haskel believed should be experienced by the congregation as a single unit; and the participants in the group must "not make a big public noise about it," so as not to offend prominent rabbinic authorities who strongly opposed women's tefillah groups. But with those caveats, he declared that "the time has come to encourage the creation of such a group in our shul."[15]

Not long afterwards, the request for permission to have a women's tefillah group was formally presented to the KJ board and approved. In its early days the group attracted 40 to 50 participants, who met once each month on Shabbat morning and proceeded with those parts of the *shacharit* and *musaf* services allowed by the Rav's guidelines. In more recent years, as interest somewhat diminished, the group convened less frequently, usually on the occasion of a bat mitzvah and on

Simchat Torah. Students at Ramaz asked for and received permission from Rabbi Lookstein to establish their own women's tefillah group. Despite the objections of some faculty members, R. Haskel ruled that the group, which met on Tuesdays, could read from the Torah, without the usual blessings, on any Tuesday when a Torah reading is mandated, such as Rosh Chodesh, Hanukkah, or a fast day.[16]

In a major address to a 1993 AMIT Women's conference on gender issues, Rabbi Lookstein spelled out in greater detail the kinds of steps he felt the Orthodox community should take in order to head off "the danger of losing the best women" and "respond to [religious] striving by women in halakhically acceptable ways." Girls and boys should not only both learn Talmud, but should learn it together. "Unless they learn it together, the better teachers will go to the boys and the weaker teachers will go to the girls. That's the way it inevitably works out. There is no such thing as separate but equal in education of the races or of the sexes." Women should daven three times daily, whether in the regular minyan or a women's tefillah group. They should also strive to be part of a *m'zumenet*, a group of three or more women who dine together and can say an introduction to *birkat hamazon* afterwards. While not recommending that women wear a tallis or tefillin, he said the Jewish community "should be understanding about it," noting that two Ramaz girls who wanted to don talleisim and tefillin were permitted to do so in the KJ morning minyan. "There is no consensus" at Ramaz in favor of letting a girl wear tallis or tefillin at the main minyan, and therefore he would not grant that permission, but he added, "I wish all of us davened with the concentration and seriousness that these young women have."[17]

In several other sermons, and in remarks delivered to a Conference on Orthodoxy and Feminism in 1998, Rabbi Lookstein outlined additional areas where he felt it was possible to be more sensitive to women's needs while not straying beyond halakhic boundaries. For example, the blessing thanking God "for not making me a woman," recited by men each morning, could be said silently so as not to offend any women at the minyan. [At KJ the practice of reciting it silently was introduced but then stopped because it created the impression the blessing was simply skipped. Instead, the problem of sensitivity to women's feelings was solved by beginning the service with the section that starts, "Rabi Ishmael omeir," after the *birkhot ha-shachar* [morning blessings, which contain the reference to women] are all said quietly. A mother's name could be included in various situations where it is commonly not mentioned, whether at a baby naming ceremony, on a *ketuba*, or on a tombstone. Women too could say the *birkat ha-gomel*, the blessing recited after a potentially dangerous journey or experience.[18]

In another area of particular concern to women, Rabbi Lookstein was an outspoken advocate of efforts to address the problem of agunot. "Rarely does a year pass for me," he wrote in 1983, "without my confronting the tragedy of a woman who is civilly divorced but whose husband, for reasons of spite, hate, avarice, or simply viciousness, refuses to free her to marry a Jew by means of granting a *get*. Similarly, with alarming frequency I share the struggle of a civilly divorced husband to encourage his former wife, sometimes estranged for a decade or more, to accept a *get* and she refuses because of the same kind of negative feelings.... In more than one case tens of thousands of dollars have been demanded by the noncompliant partner."

R. Haskel sought to confront the problem by developing a prenuptial agreement requiring the man to give a *get*, and the woman to accept it, in the event they divorce. In consultation with attorneys, he prepared a draft, which Rav Soloveitchik approved. The project received an important boost when, in a February 1983 ruling, the New York Court of Appeals ruled that such prenuptial agreements were legally binding.[19] Rabbi Lookstein decided to use the occasion of his election to a second one-year term as president of the New York Board of Rabbis, in 1987, to launch a major initiative on the agunah problem. In his address, he urged his fellow rabbis of all denominations to adopt two procedures: first, to require engaged couples to sign the prenuptial agreement; second, to impose sanctions on recalcitrant spouses, including denial of honors, synagogue membership privileges, and the right to burial in a Jewish cemetery.[20]

Rabbi Lookstein was widely applauded for his thoughtfulness and creativity, but his proposal also ran into a number of obstacles. While Conservative rabbis were generally in accord with their Orthodox colleagues on the need for a *get*, most Reform rabbis regarded the *get* as insufficiently egalitarian, since only the husband can give it. Since they disliked it in principle, they were reluctant to require it as a condition of performing a marriage ceremony. As a corollary, Reform rabbis seemed unlikely to impose sanctions on someone for failing to give a document that they did not require. Several New York area rabbis, including R. Haskel's predecessor as president of the New York Board of Rabbis, were quoted in the press as saying it was "distasteful" to discuss a prenuptial agreement about divorce conditions with a couple just before their wedding.[21]

In a series of speeches and op-ed articles in the months to follow, Rabbi Lookstein appealed to the Reform movement to compromise, explaining that the halakha simply could not be altered, and the plight of agunahs should in this case outweigh the principle of egalitarianism. As for rabbis who hesitated to raise a touchy subject on the eve of a wedding, he pointed out that "most rabbis face far more touchy situations and have to deal with them." The bottom line, he emphasized, was that there were already "between 5,000 and 15,000" Jews, mostly women, being held prisoner by vindictive former spouses. "It is irresponsible of rabbis to act as bystanders in the face of suffering. ... Do not be afraid to raise this issue with intelligent couples who are about to marry," he pleaded. "Rather be afraid of the awesome responsibility which all of us assume when we simply do nothing in the face of a growing communal problem."[22]

In response to R. Haskel's proposal, the Board of Rabbis established a committee of two Reform rabbis, two Conservative, and two Orthodox [Rabbi Lookstein and Marc Angel] to examine the issue. After many weeks of debate, the Reform members agreed to a significant compromise, accepting the principle "that as important as egalitarianism may be as a religious principle for some of us, the ability of all our children to marry freely among each other was of greater import to all of us." The committee's recommendation, adopted by the Board of Rabbis in May 1987, called on all rabbis to urge their congregants to provide a *get* in addition to civil divorce proceedings, called on synagogues to impose sanctions on recalcitrant spouses, and urged rabbis to encourage engaged couples to sign prenuptial *get* agreements—a complete victory for Rabbi Lookstein's initiative.[23] The Board's executive vice president, Rabbi Gilbert Rosenthal, characterized as "amazing" R. Haskel's success in convincing his non-Orthodox colleagues to accept his position. "It may be that only a man of Rabbi Haskel Lookstein's stature could have achieved what he did. He is truly esteemed by colleagues of all groups."[24]

Seven months later, R. Haskel received, to his surprise, a letter from the executive director of the Reconstructionist Rabbinical Association. It informed him that while the RRA could not, as a matter of principle, pledge to adhere to Orthodox strictures regarding the issue of a get, it was prepared to provide all of its member-rabbis with a list of Orthodox rabbis in major cities "who would be prepared to supervise divorce proceedings for our congregants." He predicted that "many of our members would probably refer couples to the Orthodox rabbinate if a list of competent and sensitive rabbis were made available to them." Rabbi Lookstein described the letter as "one of the most gratifying things I have ever experienced in my life.'"[25]

## NOTES

[1] Minutes of Meting of the Board of Trustees, March 25, 1971, p. 8.

[2] "Special Projects Committee, Minutes of Third Meeting, Held June 26, 1974," File: Special Projects, KJ, pp. 1–2.

[3] Arthur Silverman, Samuel Eisenstat, and Steven Gross to Rabbi Haskel Lookstein,14 August 1974, File: Special Projects, KJ.

[4] "Special Projects Committee, Minutes of Fourth Meeting, Held September 19, 1974," File: Special Projects, KJ.

[5] Rabbi Haskel Lookstein to Rabbi William Herskowitz, 24 March 1975, File: Women's Issues, KJ.

[6] Amendment to Certificate of Incorporation, for the May 6, 1976, Annual Meeting, File: Incorporation Papers, KJ.

[7] RHL Interview, 12 December 2007; "Congregation Votes in Favor of Women Trustees," KJB XLIII:14 [14 May 1976], 1; "What Is a Simchat Bat?" KJB XLIV:5 [3 December 1976], p. 4; "It Was a Great Simchat Torah!" KJB XLV:3 [14 October 1977], p. 1; "Calling Fathers [and Mothers] and Sons [and Daughters]," KJB XLVI:6 [5 January 1979], p. 2.

[8] The first was "B'not Mitzvah," KJB XLIV:3 [22 October 1976], p. 2.

[i9] Rabbi Haskel Lookstein to Ari Rath, 24 December 1986, File: Women's Issues, KJ.

[10] Rabbi Haskel Lookstein to unnamed colleagues, 25 November 1986, File: Women's Issues, KJ.

[11] Rabbi Haskel Lookstein and 19 colleagues to the *Jerusalem Post*, 15 December 1986, File: Women's Issues, KJ.

[12] The key point was that a woman could not serve as president only if "the president is authorized to spend significant sums for the congregation without clearance from an executive committee, or a board, or any other authority." [Rabbi Haskel Lookstein, Memorandum to File re: Women Being Officers in a Congregation, 28 April 1999, File: Women's Issues, KJ.]

[13] RHL Interview, 12 December 2007..

[14] RHL, "And Miriam Sang... Would She Do It Today in Queens?" [sermon], 25 January 1997, File: Sermons, KJ.

[15] RHL, "Women's Tefila Groups: Halakhic Issues and Communal Policy" [sermon], 26 March 1988, File: Sermons, KJ.

[16] Rabbi Haskel Lookstein to Participants in 11/30 Women's Tefilla Group Meeting, 2 December 1994, File: Sermons, KJ.

[17] Gitelle Rapoport, "Appeal for Understanding," *New York Jewish Week*, 14–20 January 1994; Rabbi Haskel Lookstein, "Male and Female He Created Them: A Torah Perspective on Gender Differences—Presented to AMIT Women Seminar, January 9, 1993," File: Women's Issues, KJ.

[18] Rabbi Haskel Lookstein, "Words That Hurt or Ignore Women—Panel on Liturgy," Conference on Orthodoxy and Feminism, 15 February 1998, File: Women's Issues, KJ; Rabbi Haskel Lookstein, "Dealing with Women's Issues in Ritual Matters Today—Seuda Sh'lishit—24 May 2003," File: Women's Issues, KJ.

[19] Haskel Lookstein, "The Courts Aid the Agunah," *Sh'ma*, 1983; Rabbi Haskel Lookstein to Alvin K. Hellerstein et al, 26 March 1982, File: Agunahs, KJ.

[20] William Saphire,<Au: Safire?> "Rabbis Urged to Undertake 'A Major Initiative' to Solve the Problem of Religious Divorce," Jewish Telegraphic Agency Daily News Bulletin, 26 January 1987.

[21] Stewart Ain, "Pre-marital Agreements: Clouds or Umbrellas," *Jewish World*, 19 June 1987.

[22] Haskel Lookstein, "Get Smart: Are Jews Divorced from Reality," *Jewish World* [date needed]

[23] "A Resolution of the Board of Governors of the New York Board of Rabbis for Presentation to the Membership on May 13, 1987," File: Agunahs, KJ; Haskel Lookstein, "Good News for Women Seeking Religious Divorce," *New York Jewish Week*, 20 November 1987.

[24] Rabbi Gilbert Rosenthal memoir in *Teacher, Preacher*, p. 63.

[25] Rabbi David Klatzker to Rabbi Haskel Lookstein, 19 January 1988, File: Agunahs, KJ; Rabbi Haskel Lookstein to Rabbi David Klatzker, 31 August 1988, File: Agunahs, KJ.

# VIII. THE ZIONIST

Israel and Zionism always played a major role in the life and thought of Rabbi Lookstein and the institutions he led. He grew up in a strongly Zionist home. Rabbi Joseph Lookstein was a longtime leader of the Mizrachi Religious Zionists of America and shaped the Ramaz School accordingly, with heavy emphasis on Zionist themes in the curriculum and instruction of modern Hebrew. "My father consciously selected teachers who were personally committed to the idea that Hebrew was the national tongue of the Jewish people and a central part of the Jewish national renaissance," according to R. Haskel. "That's why the teachers were so passionate about it, and their passion affected the kids." Beginning with the first bar mitzvah of a Ramaz student, in 1943, R. Joseph delivered his *d'var Torah* first in Hebrew and then in English. R. Haskel continued this tradition, not only at bar and bat mitzvahs but also at weddings of Ramaz alumni.

R. Joseph was also active, during the 1940s, in the pro-Zionist American Jewish Conference and was part of the delegation of Zionist leaders who lobbied at the 1945 founding meetings of the United Nations in San Francisco. In later years R. Joseph was active in an array of Israeli institutions, in particular Bar Ilan University, of which he was a founder and for which he served as president from 1957 to 1967 and as chancellor until 1977.

As the Zionist struggle to create a Jewish state escalated in the aftermath of the Holocaust, it became a frequent topic of discussion and concern in the Lookstein household. Haskel's summers at the strongly Zionist camp Massad were infused with activities relating to Eretz Yisrael, where Hebrew was a major part of conversation and instruction. "I lived Zionism for two months every year from 1945 through 1956," as he put it. One particular episode in the summer of 1945 deeply influenced him:

> I was 13 and a first-time camper at Massad. On Tisha B'Av night the entire camp sat on the floor in Bialik Hall, following the reading of Lamentations by candlelight. At one point Shlomo Shulsinger, director and founder of Massad, who seemed to me to be a very old man but who was probably no more than 35, began reading aggadot from the Talmud about the destruction of the Temple. He wept as he read the Aramaic words which I did not understand. But I will never forget the feeling of this "old" man shedding tears over an event that occurred 2,000 years earlier and speaking about what it meant to lose a Jewish state and how important it was that the Jewish people return to Palestine. If I had to pinpoint when Zionism became an integral part of my identity, it would be that summer night.[1]

A second transformative experience took place two decades later. Shortly after the 1967 war, Audrey proposed that they visit Israel. "I don't think you should step into the pulpit on Rosh Hashana without having seen, firsthand, what happened as a result of the war," she said. R. Haskel was concerned about the expense of the trip and agreed only reluctantly. Visiting reunited Jerusalem and newly accessible holy sites such as Rachel's Tomb, near Bethlehem, and the Cave of the Patriarchs in Hebron was, R. Haskel said later, "a profound experience, even life-altering." Seeing "the amazing transformation of Israel" was "an extremely important moment both in my professional life and in our life as a couple. Audrey was absolutely right."[2]

In an essay commemorating the centennial of the First Zionist Conference, R. Haskel made it clear that his vision of Zionism is based on the idea of "a Jewish State, not just a place where Jews might live." The difference between the two, he wrote, "is not unlike the difference between Jerusalem and Miami Beach." Israel must "clearly maintain its Jewish character." The goal of Zionism from its inception was to have a state "in which Jewish culture would thrive, the Hebrew language would be revived, and Jewish thought, religion, and traditions would predominate."[3]

Along with the mainstream of religious Zionism, Rabbi Lookstein regarded the establishment of the State of Israel as the beginning of the process leading to the messianic era, a conviction he maintained despite the turmoil of later Israeli political developments and the fragmenting of the religious Zionist community over Israeli government policies. "To be sure, the process is slow, there will be fits and starts, and one has to be patient and have faith," he wrote in 1996. "Redemption is like a little child who has to be given time grow." He noted that when Israel was founded, just 6 percent of world Jewry lived in Israel, but by 1996 that figure had grown to 33 percent. "How can this phenomenon not be considered the dawn of our redemption? But it is only the dawn, and one should not expect the sun to be shining as someday it will at high noon. That will take time, perhaps a long time, and patience is necessary."

In the wake of the 1967 Six Day War, with Israel escaping the threat of annihilation and liberating Jerusalem and other significant portions of the biblical Land of Israel, KJ adopted the Israeli chief rabbinate's decision that the *Hallel* prayer, with a full blessing, should be recited on Israel Independence Day. "Surely, there is a need to translate those miraculous deliverances into religious terminology and ritual," R. Haskel wrote in the KJ newsletter. While acknowledging that some segments of Orthodox Jewry rejected the practice as "an unnecessary pronouncement of God's name," nevertheless, "for us at Kehilath Jeshurun, the Chief Rabbi of Israel is good enough. We will take the chance based on his religious decision that praising God for the events of last year will not be viewed by God himself as taking His name in vain."[4]

Rabbi Lookstein saw in the 1990s emigration of Soviet and other Jews further evidence of the redemption process. Just ten years earlier Natan Sharansky and Yuli Edelstein were in prison; now they were members of the Israeli cabinet. Ten years earlier 5,000 Jews were suffering in Syria, 75,000 were "living in peril in Iran," and 25,000 Ethiopian Jews were "living in serfdom and bondage." By 1996 nearly all of them, along with 800,000 Soviet Jews, were living freely in Israel. "These are the living examples ... of the dawn of redemption," he wrote.[5]

To this day the Ramaz curriculum and calendar reflect the Looksteins' deep feelings about Hebrew, Zionism, and the State of Israel. The Ivrit b'Ivrit Hebrew language instruction opens up traditional Jewish source literature "while at the same time building a way to identify with *Eretz Yisrael, Medinat Yisrael,* and *Am Yisrael,*" according to R. Haskel. Jewish history classes fortify the students' connection to the biblical Land of Israel, ancient and modern. Israel Independence Day is marked with extensive celebratory activities, including the recitation of the *Hallel* thanksgiving prayer, said with all appropriate blessings, as is customary among religious Zionists. Participation in each year's Salute to Israel parade is mandatory.

As much as Ramaz's leaders were eager to have their graduates attend Ivy League universities, in the late 1970s they increasingly encouraged their students to spend a year between high school and college at a yeshiva in Israel. Indicative of the growing emphasis on spending a year in Israel is the fact that beginning in the spring of 1979 the annual front-page story in the KJ newsletter proudly listing colleges that Ramaz seniors would attend in the fall, for the first time began also announcing the names of seminaries in Israel that some of them would attend in the coming year. This new practice demonstrated both the school's pride in those students' decision and the fact that the number of students doing so had finally reached a level sufficient to merit public acknowledgment. That year 10 of the 59 graduates opted for a year in Israel.[6]

Three years later, in an overview of the school on its forty-fifth anniversary, R. Haskel noted with pride that nearly one-fourth of the senior class [up from 17 percent in 1979] "postponed college for a year to study in the finest Torah institutions in Israel. From there they will go to Princeton, Columbia, Yeshiva, Brandeis, and a host of other fine schools. But first they are deepening their Jewish commitment and learning to love Israel—the Land and the People—in a way for which they have been well prepared at Ramaz but on a level which can only be attained by living in a Torah environment in Eretz Yisrael." By 2006 nearly two-thirds of the senior class opted for a post-Ramaz year in Israel.[7]

A 1987 survey of Ramaz graduates found that 10 percent had immigrated to Israel, and 60 percent of them said their education at Ramaz had influenced their decision to make aliyah.[8] Another estimate, in 1986, calculated that 20 percent of Ramaz alumni had moved to Israel. The percentage appears to be higher among post-1967 graduates, whose exposure to Israel and Zionism was more intense than those who attended Ramaz in the 1950s and early 1960s, when interest in Israel—both at Ramaz and throughout the American Jewish community—was somewhat more subdued. Over the years R. Haskel himself did not specifically urge students to make aliyah. "I don't believe in preaching something unless I do it myself," he noted. "Israeli Army officers say, 'Acharai,' 'After me!'—not 'L'Finai,' 'You go first!' If I don't do it, I won't ask others to do it."[9]

R. Haskel's annual appeal for contributions to the United Jewish Appeal-Federation likewise always followed the "Acharai" method: he began by announcing his and Audrey's own pledge. Their annual gift had been $1,800 for some years, but it rose to $6,000 when the UJA's 1985 campaign, focusing on the airlifts of Ethiopian Jews to Israel, calculated that figure as the cost of rescuing one Ethiopian Jew. "I said to myself, how could I not contribute at least that much?" It rose to $10,000 shortly thereafter when R. Haskel became chairman of the National Rabbinic Cabinet of UJA. "I consider it my 'Jewish tax'," he explained. "It's my first responsibility, as a Jew in New York, to support what the UJA does at home and abroad." Likewise Rabbi

Lookstein's annual Israel Bond appeal began with the rabbi's announcement of his own purchase of $5,000 worth of bonds.[10]

Given Rabbi Lookstein's proclivity for public political action, it is not surprising that KJ responded to Israel's crises, such as the Six Day War and the 1973 Yom Kippur War, with rallies and vigorous fundraising campaigns, sometimes using tactics already honed in the ongoing Soviet Jewry struggle. During the 1973 war, for example, R. Haskel urged KJ members to celebrate a "present-less Hanukkah," by "taking the money that you would normally have spent on gifts and sending it as an additional contribution to the UJA Israel Emergency Fund."[11]

Other Israel-related issues in recent years that prompted KJ rallies included the extended imprisonment of Jonathan Pollard, the plight of Israeli POWs, Iranian support for terrorism, and, most notably, media bias against Israel. The *New York Times* in particular was repeatedly challenged by Rabbi Lookstein for its Mideast coverage. In the summer of 2001, in response to an article in which a *Times* reporter equated Arab terrorists and Israeli victims, Rabbis Haskel and Joshua Lookstein issued a public appeal to Jewish readers of the *Times* to suspend their subscriptions for ten days, from Rosh Hashana to Yom Kippur. "We are fed up with the bias and the distortion and are ready to do something about it," they wrote. Evidently many people agreed; R. Haskel received calls from more than 1,000 readers who said they would join the ten-day boycott. Senior editors of the *Times* quickly invited Rabbi Lookstein to a meeting, at which they admitted the newspaper had made some "mistakes." R. Haskel was not persuaded to drop his protest, but he was pleased that "someone is listening." "In the modern world with its mass societies, mass media, and mass culture, it is natural to draw the conclusion that the voice of the individual doesn't count," R. Haskel wrote later. "We feel that whatever we have to say will not be heard. Frustrated, disappointed, and resigned to our own insignificance we therefore remain silent. Recently, I learned—dramatically—that 'it ain't necessarily so.'" The *Times*' evident concern about the boycott demonstrated that protests can have an impact.[12]

In a follow-up op-ed piece in the *Jerusalem Post,* Rabbi Lookstein explained to his Israeli reading audience that the boycott of the *Times* should be regarded not only as a protest against media bias, but also as an expression of solidarity with Israel at a time when the rate of American Jewish tourism to Israel had been plummeting because of terrorism fears. "We are with you in this struggle," he wrote. "We will use our voices as effectively as we can. We will travel to Israel as often as we can. We are your family, and we recognize that when things get tough the family must respond." It was a political protest, but it was also an act of chesed. "We know that each of us has a voice. We just have to use it. Many of us are determined to do just that."[13]

Rabbi Lookstein crossed swords with the *Times* again in the spring of 2002, over the newspaper's coverage of the Passover seder massacre in Netanya and Israel's anti-terror operations in response. The *Times* further stoked the controversy when its coverage of the Salute to Israel parade featured a front-page photo of a small Arab counterdemonstration. "Is it okay to keep writing things on suffering Palestinians, who are suffering because of the terrorism of their colleagues, and not to give sufficient attention to the victims of terror?" Rabbi Lookstein asked. He urged the Jewish community to boycott the *Times* for an entire month and called upon congregations and Jewish organizations to stop placing paid death notices in the newspaper. Once again, there was an overwhelming response.[14]

The final straw came in the autumn of 2006. In a column in the *New York Jewish Week* Rabbi Lookstein announced that he had permanently canceled his subscription to the *Times,* and he explained why. Earlier that year the *Times* revealed confidential details of an ongoing U.S. government investigation into how terrorist groups receive funding through European banks. "This seemed to me, at a time when we are at war against terror, as an act bordering on sedition," he wrote. "It was quite literally an assault on the ability of the government to protect us." But it was the *Times'* reporting on the July 2006 Lebanon War that sealed R. Haskel's decision. "Throughout the war and for weeks afterwards, through pictures, headlines, and stories, the *Times* made the Lebanese and Hezbollah the victims and depicted

Israelis as disproportionate responders and murderers of civilians." At the same time, a *Times* article about rocket attacks on the Israeli town of Sderot claimed "no serious damage" was done. Rabbi Lookstein knew firsthand that the report was false; he himself had been in Sderot that week. "I saw the damage and the trauma" that the rockets had caused. "Our family has had enough," he concluded. "We will miss a lot of the wonderful features in the *Times*, but we have come to feel, regrettably, that all of its news is not necessarily fit to print--or to read."[15]

R. Haskel and the KJ-Ramaz community also spoke with their feet. In his inaugural address upon his election as president of the New York Board of Rabbis in February 1986, Rabbi Lookstein urged rabbis to lead groups from their congregations on missions to Israel as a way of showing solidarity with the Jewish state and helping its economy. The first KJ-Ramaz mission, led by Rabbi and Mrs. Lookstein, spent ten days in Israel that summer.

Four years later American Jewish tourism plummeted to a new low in the months prior to the first Gulf War. Past KJ president Sandy Eisenstadt, returning from Sukkot in Israel, reported that there were just nine guests in the King David, "a hotel," R. Haskel later noted, "where, in the past, one practically needed to know a government minister in order to get a room during the festival seasons of the year." To counter the impression among Israelis "that they are being abandoned by American Jews," Eisenstadt and Rabbi Lookstein organized a week-long mission to Israel, timed for Thanksgiving weekend so potential participants would not have to commit to missing a significant number of work days. Eighty people took part in "Operation L'Hitraot—To See and Be Seen."[16] They received an effusive welcome. A former Ramaz colleague taking the bus to work in Jerusalem heard the news of their arrival on the radio "and began to cry tears of joy." A man approached them in the hotel lobby to say, "You don't know me, but we all know you. It's great that you came. If only every rabbi would come with his congregation." The desk in Rabbi Lookstein's room was piled high with a stack of letters and messages from total strangers praising them for coming. "We saw in that enthusiastic reception the depth of pain and disappointment of our brothers and sisters in Israel. ... Every American Jew must plan to visit Israel, must talk with our feet.... Fifty years ago American Jews stood still. We cannot afford to stand still again."[17]

Ten years later, after the eruption of a second major wave of "Intifada" terrorism, Sandy Eisenstadt again returned from Sukkot in Israel to report nearly empty hotels and shuttered restaurants. Preparations for "Operation L'Hitraot II" began immediately. To those who stayed away from Israel because of perceived dangers, he responded that the real danger was not going to Israel. "If you or I were in trouble and our family avoided us, how would we feel?" he asked. "That's a real danger."[18] Sixty-seven KJ members joined that mission. In the years to follow, KJ sponsored "Operation L'Hitraot" every Thanksgiving and Pesach, often with more than 100 participants.

Another unique chesed project, undertaken in the spring of 2002, provided aid to merchants from Jerusalem's Ben Yehuda Street whose businesses had suffered as a result of the tourism drought following that year's wave of suicide bombings. On the bus ride home from a pro-Israel rally in Washington [to which KJ and Ramaz sent 1,500 people] two KJ women leaders, Riva Alper and Stacey Scheinberg, conceived of the "KJ Midrachov [the name of the pedestrians–only shopping area in downtown Jerusalem]." With Rabbi Lookstein's strong support, KJ flew seven of the Jerusalem vendors, with their stocks of merchandise, to New York City for a day of business in the 85th Street building. "Despite the rainy weather," one newspaper reported, "the first and second floors of the synagogue were wall to wall with customers all day, from 9 A.M. to 5 P.M., with 115 volunteers—men, women, and children—helping the merchants." In all, some 10,000 people came through the synagogue building that Sunday in May.

"I couldn't have imagined this in my dreams," said Jewels of Jerusalem proprietor Yuval Boteach. "For months I have not been able to pay my rent at my store, but from today alone I can pay and survive, thanks to these angels." "What this community did is unbelievable," said Uri Shkalim, owner of a women's clothing store. "Even if I had not sold one item, it would have been worth it to be here and see the outpouring of caring." All seven merchants completely sold out their wares and departed with lists of additional orders to ship. Moreover, numerous other Jewish communities in the United States and Canada, hearing of KJ's initiative, made plans to organize similar projects.[19]

Rabbi Lookstein usually steered clear of the divisive Israeli policy issues that attracted American Jewish partisans during the 1980s and 1990s. He always felt strongly that those who do not live Israel should refrain from meddling in Israeli affairs. For that reason, he responded sharply when a prominent Reform leader, Albert Vorspan, authored an essay in the *New York Times Sunday Magazine* harshly criticizing Israeli policies. R. Haskel chose to reply in the *New York Jewish Week*, since responding in the *Times* itself [even if it would allot him the space] "would be to further confuse American public opinion" by highlighting Jewish divisions. "Vorspan's job, like my job, is to support [the Israeli] government," he argued. "It is the government they chose.... It is their government and, with so much at stake, only they should be criticizing it." Vorspan's "Israel-bashing" might, "God forbid, result one day in a congressional vote" against U.S. aid to Israel, yet Vorspan, safe in his "plush Manhattan offices," would not suffer the consequences of his actions.[20]

In a similar vein, Rabbi Lookstein responded to a public attack on Israel by *Tikkun* editor Michael Lerner in 1989 with a private letter challenging Lerner's statements as "chutzpah, and dangerous." "You don't live in Israel," he wrote Lerner. "You don't take the risks that the Israelis take.... If Senators and Congressmen choose to believe you, Michael, Israel will lose financial support and military support.... [I]f something happens to the State of Israel, you ... will lose faith, pride, and all the things which we feel about Israel. But the people in Israel will lose their sons, their husbands, and perhaps many thousands of civilians."[21]

Rabbi Lookstein defended the Likud government under Yitzhak Shamir against U.S. pressure for concessions in 1988, not on the basis of whether or not the requested concessions were wise but because

"Whether all of us agree with its policies, there is an elected government in Israel [and] that government has the right to make decisions about what is best for the people of Israel." He went so far as to compare American Jewish disputes over the issue to the intra-Jewish quarrels that wracked the community during the Holocaust and undermined government support for Jewish concerns. "If there is one lesson that Jewish history has taught us, it is that Jews have to stand together when confronting danger," he argued. When we did not follow this lesson 45 years ago, we paid a terrible price. Must we pay a similar price today?"[22]

R. Haskel's search for the golden mean in Israel's political scene led him briefly to Meimad, a breakaway faction from the National Religious Party, which took positions close to his own: "centrist religious Zionism," "mutual respect and tolerance" between secular and religious Israelis, and a moderate public face for Orthodox Judaism. The fact that Meimad was founded by his personal friend Rabbi Yehuda Amital and was supported by another friend [and son-in-law of Rav Soloveitchik], Rabbi Aharon Lichtenstein, made the new party even more appealing to Rabbi Lookstein. "Never in my life have I been involved in American or Israeli politics, and I never again expect to be involved," he wrote in a private letter in 1998 supporting the new party.[23]

R. Haskel was cautiously supportive of the 1993 Oslo accords and joined Shvil Hazahav [The Golden Mean], a small group of American Orthodox Jewish intellectuals who endorsed the Israeli government's negotiating stance. This action put him at odds with much of the U.S. Orthodox rabbinate, where sentiment toward the Oslo accords generally ranged from skepticism to fervent opposition. In the wake of continued Arab terrorism, however, Rabbi Lookstein in May 1995 urged Israel to suspend its negotiations with the Palestinian Authority, arguing that the Jewish State would become a "prisoner of the peace process" if it made additional concessions despite the PA's failure to act against terror groups. By 1997 he had concluded that "the Arabs do not want peace," although by that time a Likud government was in power, so his position was once again supportive of the Israeli govern-ment.[24] On the other hand, reports that the Labor government would in 2001 divide Jerusalem prompted Rabbi Lookstein to host a public rally at KJ, at which he spoke against giving over any parts of the city to Arab rule.[25]

Somewhat paradoxically, the rabbinical sage whom R. Haskel has since the 1990s cited as his most important intellectual mentor after his father and Rav Solovetichik, is an Israeli rabbi who holds views on political and territorial issues far more nationalistic than his own: Rabbi Shlomo Aviner, head of the Ateret Yerushalayim [formerly known as Ateret Cohanim] yeshiva in Jerusalem's Old City. For R. Haskel, Rabbi Aviner's opposition to any Israeli surrender of territory is secondary in importance to his profound commitment to the prin-ciples of *derech eretz* [good manners] and *ahavat Yisrael* [love of fellow-Jews], which R. Haskel regarded as nearly identical to the philosophy of "menschliness before Godliness" that he himself always espoused.[26]

# NOTES

[1] *Hadassah Magazine*, December 1997

[2] RHL interview, 13 February 2008.

[3] Haskel Lookstein, "Israel: A Jewish State," *The Reporter* [Women's American ORT], May 1997, p. 42.

[4] Haskel Lookstein, "A Religion Which Addresses Our Needs," KJB XXXVI:33 [24 May 1968] p. 2.

[5] Rabbi Haskel Lookstein, "I Say the Prayer for the State of Israel," undated [1996], File: Religious Zionism, KJ. The sermon was based on a poem by Rabbi Shlomo Aviner.

[6] Compare "Ramaz Seniors Establish Outstanding Record as School Completes 41st Year," KJB XLV:12, 2 June 1978, p. 1—the last such article to refrain from men-tioning students going to Israel—to "Ramaz to Graduate 59 Seniors on June 13; Ten Complete Their Studies in Israel," KJB XLVI:11 [31 May 1979], p. 1, inaugurating the inclusion of Israeli yeshivot, a practice that continues to this day.

[7] Rabbi Haskel Lookstein, "Looking Back and Ahead: A View of Ramaz at Age 45" [New York: Ramaz,1982].

[8] Nathalie Friedman, "The Graduates of Ramaz: Fifty Years of Jewish Day School Education," in Jeffrey S. Gurock, ed., *Ramaz: School, Community, Scholarship and Orthodoxy* [Hoboken, N.J.: Ktav, 1989], pp. 83–123.

[9] Greer Fay Cashman, "Manhattan's Ramaz Orthodox School Celebrates Its Fiftieth Anniversary," *Jerusalem Post*, 29 August 1986.

[10] RHL interview, 12 December 2007.

[11] "More Than Half a Million Raised for Israel by Kehilath Jeshurun Members," KJB XXXV:32 [9 June 1967], p. 1; Haskel Lookstein, "A 'Presentless Chanukah' This Year?" KJB XLI:7 [7 December 1973], p, 1.

[12] RHL, 12 December 2007; Haskel Lookstein and Joshua Lookstein, "Sending a Message to the N.Y.Times," *New York Jewish Week*, 15 June 2001; "The Rabbi Meets the Editor," *New York Jewish Week*, 13 July 2001; Haskel Lookstein, "Your Voice Does Count," unpublished op-ed, July 2001, File: Zionism, KJ.

[13] Haskel Lookstein, "The Worst of 'Times," and How to Fight It," *Jerusalem Post*, 5 August 2001.

[14] Felicity Barringer, "Some U.S. Backers of Israel Boycott Dailies Over Mideast Coverage that They Deplore," *New York Times*, 23 May 2002.

[15] Rabbi Haskel Lookstein, "No More Time for 'The Times,'" *New York Jewish Week*, 15 September 2006.

[16] Haskel Lookstein, "Why You and I Must Go to Jerusalem Now" [op-ed], 23 November 1990.

[17] Haskel Lookstein, "Talking with Their Feet," *Jerusalem Post*, 4 December 1990.

[18] Haskel Lookstein, "The Danger In Not Going to Israel," *New York Jewish Week*, 15 December 2000.

[19] Gary Rosenblatt, "Buying Israeli, First Hand," *New York Jewish Week*, 17 May 2002.

[20] Haskel Lookstein, "Public Policy Debate Rests with Israelis," *New York Jewish Week*, 27 May 1988.

[21] Haskel Lookstein to Michael Lerner, 8 March 1989, File: Israel, KJ; Lerner to Lookstein, 25 April 1989, File: Israel, KJ; Lookstein to Lerner, 8 May 1989, File: Israel, KJ. Lerner responded by accusing Rabbi Lookstein of not having "the slightest understanding of Torah or the Prophets."

[22] Rabbi Haskel Lookstein, "Doomed to Watch History Repeat Itself," *New York Jewish Week*, 8 April 1988, p. 22; also see Rabbi Haskel Lookstein, "A Time to Be Silent and a Time to Speak Out," *New York Jewish Week*, 28 October 1988, p. 26.

[23] Rabbi Haskel Lookstein to "Dear Friends," 11 October 1988, KJ; Rabbi Haskel Lookstein to Members of Kehilath Jeshurun, 15 November 1988, File: Meimad, KJ.

[24] RHL interview, 12 December 2007; Richard Bernstein, "For Jews in America, a Time for New Hope and New Fear," *New York Times*, 3 September 1993; Haskel Lookstein, "Prisoners of Peace, No!" *Jewish World*, 12–18 May 1995; Rabbi Haskel Lookstein, "Ghosts of Destruction," *New York Jewish Week*, 8 August 1997.

[25] Hundreds Gather in NY for Pro-Jerusalem Rally," *Jerusalem Post*, 9 January 2001.

[26] RHL interview, 12 February 2008. A second Israeli scholar whom R. Haskel regards as a major intellectual influence on him was Nechama Liebowitz, whose shiurim he attended in Jerusalem on many occasions, and whose methods for studying Chumash he closely follows.

# IX. CENTRIST ORTHODOXY

During the 1970s and 1980s there were increasing indications that a segment of the American Orthodox community was becoming stricter in its religious observance and less tolerant of those who were not as strict. This trend was evidently due to factors such as *ba'alei teshuva* undertaking particularly rigorous observance, modern Orthodox adolescents "rebelling" by becoming more punctilious than their parents, and a growing resentment in the Orthodox community toward the permissiveness of American culture. The shift toward more rigorous observance and separatist attitudes became apparent in areas such as modes of attire, standards of kashrut, choice of schools, and attitudes toward non-Orthodox Jews and non-Jews. Rabbi Lookstein and like-minded colleagues half-jokingly chracterized these trends as a "*chumrah* of the month club," referring to individuals who believed it was religiously advisable to abide by nonobligatory strictures. R. Haskel, by contrast, advocated Centrist Orthodoxy, that is, an Orthodoxy anchored in openness to American culture and a desire to cooperate with other wings of Judaism and members of other faiths. Moreover, he argued that centrism was not merely a default position of quietly refraining from extremism, but rather a principle that needed to be advocated with vigor. "We must be passionate about our centrism," he asserted in one 1987 appeal. Referring to recent clashes between Orthodox and secular militants in Israel, he wrote: "Today, while the extremists are passionate, the centrists are passive. No more! We must be insistent about *ahavat chinam* [unconditional love] in the face of *sinat chinam* [unwarranted hatred] which threatens to destroy us."[1]

For many years the Synagogue Council of America served as a battleground in the struggle between Orthodox separatists and Orthodox advocates of cooperation. As early as 1983, separatist elements within the generally centrist Union of Orthodox Jewish Congregations of America [OU] pressed, behind the scenes, for withdrawal of the OU from the Synagogue Council. They contended that the OU's participation in the Synagogue Council constituted de facto Orthodox recognition of the legitimacy of the non-Orthodox groups in the council. Rabbi Lookstein strongly supported Orthodox participation in the council, as did his father, who served a term as its president. "The Synagogue Council of America serves both symbolically and functionally to emphasize the unity that transcends our divisions and the solidarity of the Jewish people that takes precedence over any disagreements," R. Haskel wrote in one of many letters to the OU leadership, urging them to reject the mindset of those Orthodox Jews "who have turned inward to such an extent that the concerns of Klal Yisrael [the Jewish People] are not theirs any more. They only find time to criticize, not to support, to disparage other Jews and not to join with other Jews in helping to save Jewish lives." To reinforce Rabbi Lookstein's position, the 1985 annual meeting of Kehilath Jeshurun adopted a resolution that expressed strong support for the OU's continuing to be part of the Synagogue Council. The persistence of rumors of a possible OU withdrawal from the council eventually compelled R. Haskel to warn its leaders bluntly that if they took such a step he would "vote with my pocketbook and with my congregation's pocketbook as well," by withdrawing Kehilath Jeshurun from the OU and working to establish "a new Synagogue Council affiliated with Yeshiva University.[2]

Signs of Orthodox intolerance seemed to be multiplying. On the eve of the High Holidays in 1984, the Agudas Harabonim, a small association of separatist Orthodox rabbis, placed an advertisement in several New York Jewish newspapers, declaring it better to refrain from attending synagogue altogether on Rosh Hashana or Yom Kippur than to go to a non-Orthodox synagogue. Rabbi Lookstein denounced the ad as a "slap [in] the faces of Reform and Conservative Jews" and an attempt to cause them "pain and embarrassment." If the ad's sponsors thought their pronouncement would prevent Jews from committing a sin, they were utterly mistaken, he wrote. "Nobody responds to such teaching. No one responded to it when it was the fashion in Eastern Europe fifty years ago."[3] Moreover, he explained in a later op-ed article in the *Jewish Week*, it was wrong to "attack the validity of non-Orthodox movements" when those movements in fact play a positive role in Jewish life. A Reform Jew "attending a temple service on the Sabbath, even if that service does not conform to halakhic standards" was clearly better than that Jew "spending that morning on the golf course or at the beach." An egalitarian religious service "is in my view counter to halakha," but "if the Jewish identity of a Conservative Jew is strengthened" by taking part in such a service, surely that is "positive for that particular Jew" and better than having him or her "assimilate and not step inside any synagogue." While "of course we would hope that people would embrace the entirety of Shabbat, without a question half a challah is better than none. Such an approach does not repel Jews but rather attracts them. In the long run, there will be more Jews, a heightened Jewish identity, and a greater sense of belonging to a people by virtue of [this approach] than through the demanding proclamations of the Agudas Harabonim."[4]

Additional signs of intolerance abounded. In one instance a prominent Orthodox rabbi who was invited to be honored along with the community's other rabbis at a UJA fundraising dinner said he would attend only if he were listed separately from the non-Orthodox rabbis in the program and seated on a dais that was physically separate from that of the other rabbis.[5] Meanwhile, shortly before Rabbi Alexander Shapiro, president of the [Conservative] Rabbinical Assembly addressed the [Orthodox] Rabbinical Council of America in the spring of 1985, some wives of RCA rabbis received a letter from

Orthodox critics urging them to influence their husbands to boycott the event. The letter asserted that the participation of a Conservative rabbi qualified as a desecration of God's name. Rabbi Lookstein, by contrast, not only rejected such views but himself spoke at the Rabbinical Assembly's annual convention in 1995, and even addressed the attendees as "my dear fellow and sister rabbis."[6]

The rotation agreement by which rabbis of different denominations take turns as president of the New York Board of Rabbis by chance resulted in Rabbi Lookstein's elevation to the presidency precisely in the midst of these controversies. He decided to use his inaugural address, in December 1985, to focus attention on the issue of Jewish unity and to propose a possible solution. "[T]he growing polarization that exists in the religious community both here and in Israel" poses "a serious and frightening threat" to the Jewish people, he said. "So many of us are unable to speak to each other civilly. Religious rightists and leftists throw epithets at each other. The extremism that manifests itself on both sides threatens to isolate Jew from Jew and to rend the fabric of Jewish peoplehood so that we will no longer be one people."

Noting the relatively small number of Orthodox rabbis involved in the Board of Rabbis, Rabbi Lookstein bemoaned the fact that "so many of my Orthodox colleagues ... want no part of dialogue" with the non-Orthodox. But, he emphasized, there had been statements and actions by the left—by Reform leaders—that were just as unreasonable as those from the right. The 1982 Reform decision to accept as Jewish anyone who has one Jewish parent, whether it is the mother or father, "threatens to tear us apart as a people, because we will no longer have a common ground for agreement on who is Jewish and who is not."

R. Haskel's solution was multifold. To improve the general atmosphere in the Jewish community, he called on both sides to undertake a general "lowering of the strident tones of our rhetoric." He asked Orthodox rabbis "to extend a hand of friendship and love to Conservative and Reform rabbis and not to be afraid to sit down with them" to discuss issues of contention. He asked his Conservative and

Reform colleagues to take three specific steps to promote Jewish unity: reconsideration of the decision on one-parent Jewish identity [patrilineal descent]; cooperation in finding a method of converting non-Jews to Judaism that would be acceptable to all denominations, including the Orthodox; and acceptance of the principle that every Jewish divorce should be done in a way "that will be acceptable to the Jewish people as a whole," that is, through a *get*. If it seemed that his prescription for unity was somewhat unbalanced, asking the Conservative and Reform rabbis to take specific steps while asking the Orthodox for something that was "rather unspecific," that would be a mistaken impression, Rabbi Lookstein wrote. In fact, "such a change in attitude on the part of the Orthodox establishment"—a willingness to engage in dialogue with the non-Orthodox on religious issues—"would constitute a very significant shift in outlook." The publication of most of R. Haskel's address in the pages of *Moment* magazine shortly afterwards helped bring his proposals to even wider public attention.[7]

As noted above, Rabbi Lookstein subsequently used his address upon reelection as head of the Board of Rabbis in early 1987 to focus even more energetically on the get issue in particular. That stance resulted in the decision of an intradenominational committee in favor of accepting the principle of insisting on a *get* and sanctioning recalcitrant spouses. But when he announced this victory at the May 1987 RCA convention, R. Haskel received what he considered "a very lukewarm reception." From his perspective, he was "bringing to them a tremendous accomplishment ... that indicated the willingness of Reform and Conservative rabbis to meet us on our own terms" on the *get* issue. "I have persuaded an organization, composed of at least two-thirds non-Orthodox rabbis, to approve and endorse the obtaining of a *get* by everybody who gets a civil divorce," he pointed out. "Surely this has to be considered a positive result of intergroup cooperation." Evidently not, he discovered. "Unfortunately, the accomplishment was not deemed terribly worthy by my colleagues. It was a depressing experience. But it was probably a necessary awakening for me" in that it illustrated for him how far separatist attitudes were penetrating modern Orthodoxy.[8]

Much to Rabbi Lookstein's chagrin, the issue of relations between Orthodox and non-Orthodox Jews suddenly assumed international dimensions after the Israeli parliamentary election of November 1988. The victorious Likud's ability to form a governing coalition depended on four Orthodox parties, which conditioned their participation on amending the Law of Return to recognize a convert to Judaism only if the conversion were performed according to halakha. Although in practical terms the legislation would have affected only the small number of non-Orthodox converts who sought to immigrate to Israel, it would have enshrined in Israeli law the principle that the State of Israel did not recognize non-Orthodox conversions as legitimate. American Reform and Conservative leaders flew to Israel to lobby Prime Minister Yitzhak Shamir and his colleagues against the amendment. Rabbi Lookstein joined them. R. Haskel has always believed "that Americans should not be making decisions for Israelis," but "this time Israelis were making decisions for Americans." As a result, "we had every right—indeed, obligation—to take a very strong position" against the amendment.[9] For him the issue was not the halakhic validity of non-Orthodox conversions, which he too could not accept. Rather, what troubled Rabbi Lookstein was the pain that the amendment would cause to large numbers of non-Orthodox Jews, the strains that it would create in the relations between Orthodox and non-Orthodox Jews, and the image of intolerance that would be attached to Orthodox Judaism.

Expecting Israeli officials to be less sensitive to those concerns than to the danger of an anti-Israel backlash, the delegation stressed that "if the State of Israel rejects a large body of people who consider themselves as Jews, those people may very well reject the State of Israel and repudiate our national homeland.... The results in terms of financial support of Israel and, more importantly, political support, could very well be disastrous for our people and for the State of Israel.... No Israeli leader should expose Israel to such a possible loss of support and to the alienation of hundreds of thousands who, being rejected, will react in the manner in which any rejected person would react."[10]

As for the question of how the Israeli government should relate to non-Orthodox converts seeking to be recognized as Jews, "there is no need for a secular government in Israel to deal with these Halakhic issues." They should be "left to the chief rabbinate, which has experience in resolving those problems which may arise from time to time," such as when a non-Orthodox convert in Israel seeks permission to marry a Jew. Indeed, if he himself were asked to perform a marriage involving such a person, "I would have to face the Halakhic questions regarding their Jewishness" just as the chief rabbinate does, but that could be handled quietly on an individual basis, presumably involving some sort of conversion process acceptable to Orthodoxy.

Drawing on his research about American Jewish responses to the Holocaust, Rabbi Lookstein noted that negotiations between American Zionist and non-Zionist leaders to establish a joint fundraising apparatus foundered in October 1938 when the non-Zionists broke off the talks. A few weeks later the Kristallnacht pogrom devastated German Jewry, and the shaken non-Zionists quickly concluded an agreement for establishment of the United Palestine Appeal [later called the United Jewish Appeal]. "What a tragic irony," R. Haskel commented, if "just weeks after the fiftieth anniversary of the terrible pogrom of Kristallnacht the unity of the Jewish people which Kristallnacht created would be dissipated and our people would be torn apart by anger and resentment."[11]

In this controversy too Rabbi Lookstein sought the golden mean, opposing the amendment but also repudiating the "exaggerations and Orthodox-bashing" by some anti-Orthodox elements.[12] He was particularly troubled by a sermon in which Stanley Davids, a Reform rabbi who was part of the delegation to Israel, attacked "the narrow-minded bigotry of 770 Eastern Parkway," headquarters of the Lubavitch movement, which favored amending the Law of Return. The Lubavitcher Rebbe "is a warm, loving Jew ... a saintly, deeply religious man, not a narrow-minded bigot," Rabbi Lookstein responded.

"It is this kind of Orthodox-bashing which is angering many modern Orthodox rabbis and making the effort to bring us together much more difficult."[13]

R. Haskel also took the opportunity of his exchange with Rabbi Davids to reiterate the importance of leaders from each denomination challenging their own congregants rather than focusing criticism on other groups, a point he had made on numerous occasions. "When I speak in my shul, I blast my own group," he wrote to Rabbi Davids. "I do not talk about what Reform Judaism has done to deeply divide the American Jewish community. I do not blast [Reform leader] Alex Schindler. Rather, I criticize my own colleagues for not being ready to sit down with Alex Schindler and work out a solution to our problems." He urged Davids to likewise spend his time "educating your congregation about the flaws in your own camp rather than inflaming them about the rather obvious and troubling problems in the camps of others." Doing so might result in criticism from some of his congregants, R. Haskel acknowledged, but then, he added, quoting Rabbi Israel Salanter, the famed nineteth-century founder of the Mussar movement, "A rabbi whom everybody likes is not a rabbi."[14]

Rabbi Lookstein made the same point some time later when Rabbi Ismar Schorsch, then chancellor of the Jewish Theological Seminary, publicly alleged that modern Orthodoxy was being overtaken by "the escalating power of ultra-Orthodox values" such as stricter criteria for conversions and taller *mechitzas* to separate men and women during prayer services. "I wonder why it is necessary for the head of the Conservative movement to pound away at the far right in Orthodoxy," R. Haskel wrote him. "I don't pound away at the far left in Conservative Judaism, and there certainly is a far left. That is a Conservative problem; the far right here in America is largely an Orthodox problem.... This is our struggle, not yours."[15]

Despite their occasional disagreements, Rabbi Lookstein found over the years that there was "a tremendous advantage" to associating with rabbis of other movements. For him, pluralism—which he mockingly called "the P word," to indicate the disdain in which it is held in some Orthodox circles—was not a concession but a valuable experience. "I learned a lot from their perspective, and they from mine," he said. "It was mutually edifying. You naturally develop more respect for people with whom you disagree when you meet face to face." R. Haskel recalled his experiences as a leader of the New York Board of Rabbis and the UJA's Rabbinic Cabinet as "exciting, informative, and in certain ways even formative—for my understanding of the ways other Jews see things."[16]

With his deeply held philosophy of intra-Jewish tolerance and his appreciation for the benefits of interaction with all Jewish denominations, Rabbi Lookstein was well suited for the presidency of the Synagogue Council of America, just as his father had been fifteen years earlier. However, by the time the system of presidential rotation gave R. Haskel the opportunity to serve, the council was beset with institutional troubles. Although it was established [in 1926] for the purpose of fostering unity among American Jewry's religious denominations, its member-organizations came to realize that their theological differences made it too difficult to find substantive common ground. As a result, the council's main function for many years had been to represent U.S. Jewry in dealing with the representative bodies of other religions. That would have constituted a useful occupation except that other, better-funded Jewish organizations such as the Anti-Defamation League and the American Jewish Committee established their own relationships with an array of religious agencies and leaders. In his September 1993 installation address, Rabbi Lookstein acknowledged that the work of the council had come to focus on "the outside world," but he pledged to strive also for "a higher purpose: to demonstrate how harmoniously we can work together, blending our voices in a symphony of tolerance and understanding rather than creating a cacophony of dissonance by mutual disrespect and mistrust."[17]

Few of R. Haskel's colleagues at the Synagogue Council shared his enthusiasm. Even his mild suggestion for a pre-Rosh Hashana campaign urging every Jew to join a synagogue failed to win approval. The Orthodox groups rejected it on the grounds that the plan was religious in nature, and as a matter of principle they rejected the council's right to play a role in Jewish religious affairs. The Reform and Conservative movements, for their part, insisted that such a campaign was the responsibility of their own congregational associations, not the SCA as a whole.[18] R. Haskel's vision of tolerance and cooperation was colliding with the reality of the member-groups' rapidly dwindling interest in the work of the council and the financial debt the council had accumulated in recent years, which was approaching $200,000. Unable to meet its basic expenses, the council closed down in November 1994.[19]

The struggle over relations between the Orthodox and non-Orthodox soon erupted anew on, of all places, New York City's basketball courts. In 1996 a Solomon Schechter [Conservative] day school applied to join an all-Orthodox basketball league, the Metropolitan Jewish High School League. Administered by a council of principals of the participating day schools, under the auspices of the Greater New York Board of Jewish Education, the league was the framework for basketball competition among Jewish schools in the New York City area. In the discussions within the Principals' Council about the application, opposition to admitting Schechter coalesced around two concerns: that granting it admission would be tantamount to recognizing the legitimacy of Conservative Judaism, and that interaction with boys or girls who were less observant could have a negative influence on the yeshiva students.

R. Haskel, as the Ramaz representative on the Principals' Council, made the case in support of admitting Schechter. Instead of offering a tactical argument, that playing sports with a Conservative school did not constitute recognition of Conservative Judaism, or that opportunities for social interaction at the games were minimal, Rabbi Lookstein decided to take a stand on the principle of cooperation. He argued that the primary concern of day school principals should be to ensure that all Jewish children receive a Jewish education, and while an Orthodox education was desirable, Schechter and other non-Orthodox schools constituted "a very good alternative" for those families that would otherwise opt to send their children to secular schools.

His argument was not well received. Moreover, the discussion grew heated, with both sides making remarks that R. Haskel later characterized as "angry, vituperative, and frankly disrespectful." Tempers calmed down only after Rabbi William Altshul, then principal of the Yeshiva of Flatbush, rose and declared, "I don't think this is the kind of meeting at which the Chofetz Chaim would have felt comfortable, and if this doesn't stop, I'm walking out." Tempers cooled, but when the application was put to a vote, the separatists carried the day: the overwhelming majority of the approximately two dozen council members rejected Schechter's application, with only Rabbi Lookstein and a few other principals dissenting. For R. Haskel it was further evidence that the separatist mood was spreading within American Orthodoxy.

Rabbi Lookstein was not, however, prepared to let the matter lie. His persistence may or may not have been influenced in part by his own well-known affection for sports. Rabbi Lookstein's passion for tennis is often remarked upon among KJ members; his fondness for New York's baseball, basketball, football, and hockey teams is so fervent that he sometimes videotapes their games when they conflict with his schedule, in order to watch them late at night while exercising on his treadmill; and even in his 70s he can still sink his patented two-handed set shot in the annual Ramaz faculty–student basketball game. R. Haskel's enthusiasm for Ramaz's sports teams is such that he has often attended their matches wearing a team jersey. Add to all that his strong views on the issue of cooperation between Orthodox and non-Orthodox Jews and it was perhaps inevitable that he would not easily concede defeat in the Metropolitan Jewish High School League affair.

Convinced that the Jewish community had "enough things that divide us ideologically without being divided athletically," Rabbi Lookstein and like-minded colleagues from two other Orthodox day schools announced that they would establish an alternative league together with three area Schechter schools. Theirs would be a league that would uphold the value of Jewish unity. Moreover, by demonstratively spurning the exclusionist trend within Orthodoxy, the new league would project a kinder, gentler image of Orthodoxy to the non-

Orthodox world, a longtime Lookstein goal. Despite its noble intentions, the alternative league lasted just one season, because the three dissident Orthodox schools simultaneously remained part of the MJHSL, and it proved too stressful for the students to play a full schedule of games in two leagues at once. The controversy, however, was far from over.

The following year the Schechter schools' petition was again turned down by the league, but this time Schechter supporters decided to take their case to the United Jewish Appeal-Federation of Greater New York, the financial sponsor of the Board of Jewish Education. After four years of lobbying, UJA officials eventually agreed, in 2001, to threaten to withhold funding from the board unless the basketball policy was changed. The Principals' Council responded by voting to break the league away from the Board of Jewish Education. Rabbi Lookstein and his allies, for their part, announced that they would try again to create their own league unless the policy of exclusion was canceled. Another round of behind-the-scenes negotiations ensued, and in May 2001 a compromise was announced. The non-Orthodox schools would be permitted to play in the league on condition that their home games would not be played in their schools, and that Orthodox rabbis would rule on any "matters of halakha" that might arise in connection with the games. Ironically, however, after struggling for so many years to gain admission to the league, only one of the Schechter schools actually joined the league. The others refused on the grounds that they did not accept the right of Orthodox rabbis to have the last word in matters of dispute.[20]

One of the next great battlegrounds in the struggle between the factions within Orthodoxy will likely be the issue of conversions, another area in which Rabbi Lookstein took a substantial interest in recent years. R. Haskel's approach to the issue of converting non-Jews to Judaism was shaped both by his own vision of Orthodoxy as open and welcoming, and by a specific reply that Rav Soloveitchik gave him to the question of how demanding a rabbi should be in deciding whether to convert an applicant. "The Rav's answer was that one should never ask a convert to promise to do a specific mitzvah, because if the answer is no, you cannot go any further in the conversion process," he recalled. "The convert's acceptance of the 613 mitzvas is a general commitment, not a specific reference to any one particular commandment." The rule of thumb, Rav Soloveitchik explained, was that "the rabbi has to be reasonably convinced that the would-be convert is going to lead an observant Jewish life." In recent years, however, a growing number of younger rabbis have adopted a different position, insisting that the potential convert commit in advance, quite specifically, to a fully observant lifestyle. Rabbi Lookstein, by contrast, follows his father's approach. "He would ask a prospective convert, 'Have you come here to embrace Judaism or to embrace a Jew?' If, out of a desire to embrace a Jew—that is, their future spouse—the person is ready to embrace Judaism, then you have to give him or her every opportunity to proceed."

The Lookstein position appears to be in the minority in the Orthodox world. In 2005 the Office of the Sephardic Chief Rabbi of Israel for the first time raised questions about the validity of Orthodox conversions performed in the United States. "There were a handful of instances in which Orthodox rabbis may have proceeded too hastily in converting someone," according to R. Haskel. "But it was a small problem which could have been resolved quietly, on an individual basis." Instead the chief rabbinate called for creation of a single, centralized system of conversions according to strict criteria, to be administered by the Rabbinical Council of America. R. Haskel was a member of the commission appointed by the RCA to examine the chief rabbinate's request. He argued that if Orthodox rabbis adopted unnecessarily strict standards, prospective converts will go to Reform or Conservative rabbis for their conversions and then affiliate with those movements. In the end, however, his was a lone voice of dissent; even the few other commission members who privately agreed with R. Haskel refrained from voicing their views. The commission endorsed the rabbinate's stance, and in late 2007 the RCA agreed to require its members to abide by the more rigorous criteria for conversions.

A similar problem will soon arise with regard to the conversion of the adopted children of nonobservant couples, according to Rabbi Lookstein. "If we tell the parents that their home must be kosher and Shomer Shabbos and they must live within walking distance of an Orthodox synagogue, they will not have their child undergo an Orthodox conversion." The result is that the child will receive a Conservative or Reform conversion, and his Jewishness will be recognized by everyone in the Jewish community except the Orthodox. "It's embarrassing to Orthodoxy, and unfair to the couple," in R. Haskel's view. "They have just gone through the agony of infertility and the adoption process, and we are closing the door in their face. We have to remember that 'love thy neighbor as thyself' includes loving nonobservant Jews who have suffered with infertility." Here too the Rav's advice to him was particularly helpful: try to get the parents to be as observant as possible, but the main requirement is that they commit to give the child a Jewish education [i.e., day school]. If they make that commitment, the child can be converted.[21]

## NOTES

[1] RHL, "It's Time to Turn Things Around," KJB LV:1 [18 September 1987], p. 1.

[2] Haskel Lookstein to Julius Berman, 7 December 1983, File: Synagogue Council of America, KJ; Haskel Lookstein to Sidney Kwestel, 1 April 1985, File: Synagogue Council of America, KJ; Haskel Lookstein to Sidney Kwestel, 6 May 1985, File: Synagogue Council of America, KJ; "Resolution on the Involvement of the Union of Orthodox Jewish Congregations of America in the Synagogue Council of America," 1 May 1985, File: Synagogue Council of America, KJ; Haskel Lookstein to Sidney Kwestel, 11 March 1987, File: Synagogue Council of America, KJ; Haskel Lookstein to Sidney Kwestel, 28 May 1987, File: Synagogue Council of America, KJ.

[3] Haskel Lookstein, "An Orthodox Response to an Unorthodox Ad," *New York Jewish Week*, 19 October 1994.

[4] Haskel Lookstein, "An Orthodox Response to an UnOrthodox Charge," *New York Jewish Week*, 4 April 1997.

[5] Rabbi Haskel Lookstein to Rabbi Marc Angel, 7 May 1985, KJ; Haskel Lookstein, "Mending the Rift: A Proposal," *Moment*, March 1986, p. 59.

[6] Rabbi Haskel Lookstein and Rabbi Alan Silverstein, "Denominational Jews: Do Our Titles Really Define Us?" Proceedings of the 1995 Convention of The Rabbinical Assembly, p.5.

[7] "Remarks Prepared for Delivery by Rabbi Haskel Lookstein at Annual Meeting of the New York Board of Rabbis , Wednesday, December 18, 1985, 11:00 A.M.," File: Pluralism, KJ; "Mending the Rift," op.cit

[8] Rabbi Haskel Lookstein to Rabbi Binyamin Walfish, 20 May 1987, File: Law of Return, KJ; Rabbi Haskel Lookstein to Sidney Kwestel, 28 May 1987, File: Law of Return, KJ.

[9] Rabbi Haskel Lookstein to Dr. MIchael Wyschogrod, 28 February 1989, File: Law of Return, KJ.

[10] Haskel Lookstein, "We Are One and We Will Remain One: An Orthodox Response to a Political Crisis," undated [November 1987], KJ.

[11] Ibid.

[12] Rabbi Haskel Lookstein to Dr. and Mrs. Elmer Offenbacher, 15 December 1988, File: Pluralism, KJ.

[13] Rabbi Haskel Lookstein to Rabbi Stanley M. Davids, 5 January 1989, File: Pluralism, KJ.

[14] Ibid.

[15] E. J. Kessler, "Schorsch Touches Nerve with Broadside," Forward, 24 July 1998, p. 3.

[16] RHL, "Religious Pluralism—An Unorthodox Orthodox View—Adapted from a Presentation to the American Jewish Committee, Tuesday, December 10, 1996," File: Pluralism, KJ.

[17] "Installation Address, Synagogue Council of America, September 20, 1993, by Haskel Lookstein," File: Synagogue Council of America, KJ, p. 2.

[18] RHL interview, 19 November 2007.

[19] Steve Lipman, "Seeking Common Ground," New York Jewish Week, 24–30 September 1993; Debra Nussbaum Cohen, 'Synagogue Council Succumbs to Financial Ills," Jewish World, 2–8 December 1994; Rabbi Haskel Lookstein to The Agency Executives of the Member Organizations of the Synagogue Council of America, 10 October 1994, File: Synagogue Council of America, KJ.

[20] Jeffrey S. Gurock, Judaism's Encounter with American Sports [Bloomington: Indiana University Press, 2005], pp. 177–180; RHL interview, 21 January 2008.

[21] RHL interview, 23 January 2008.

# X. THE TEACHER

Rabbi Joseph Lookstein privately suspected that his son's real reason for becoming assistant rabbi at KJ was to afford him the opportunity "to express his primary love, which was Jewish education."[1] There certainly appears to be at least a grain of truth in that suspicion. As soon as R. Haskel began at KJ in 1959, he began teaching Tanach and Talmud at Ramaz. Within two years he was named Coordinator of Judaic Studies for the high school and was teaching Talmud, Chumash, Prophets, and American Jewish history. "He proved to be a gifted teacher who not only loved to teach but also loved the children whom he taught," R. Joseph noted in 1978. "Even now, when he is preoccupied with so many duties, I can still 'catch' him in the room adjoining his office surreptitiously teaching several boys how to chant the service as officiating cantors. As I look in on him, there is a sly smile on his face which seems to say, 'I know I'm cheating, but I love to do this.'"[2]

The Talmud course that he taught to sophomores in his first year was especially memorable. "I gave them the full gamut of my experience in learning Tractate Beitza with the Rav," he noted. "It was a fabulous class, lively and interesting for both them and me." It also provided an early experience in nascent Orthodox feminism. At the time, girls would learn Talmud only through tenth grade and then take typing and home economics in their final two years. "There was a certain

1950s logic behind this structure," he concedes. "How could a girl get a job in those days if she couldn't type? And how could she run a household if she couldn't cook?" But toward the end of the year two girls from R. Haskel's class, Vivian Eisenberg and Shira Neiman, asked the upper school headmaster for permission to continue studying Talmud in the year ahead. "The glass ceiling was broken," R. Haskel recalls. "I was proud that their experience learning Talmud with me contributed to their desire to continue." Their initiative changed the rules; girls were henceforth given the option to study Talmud in eleventh and twelfth grades. Today it is no longer an option; girls are expected to achieve the same prowess in Talmud as the boys. R. Haskel points with pride to the fact that Vivian and Shira proved to be exceptionally successful in the professional world as well. Vivian earned a Ph.D. in art history and today holds the Feld Chair in Judaica at the Jewish Museum; Shira, an attorney, became the first woman in the criminal division of the U.S. Attorney's Office. They exemplify the type of student that R. Joseph, and his son after him, have wanted Ramaz to produce: one who is comfortable and accomplished in both Orthodoxy and the broader community.

In 1967 R. Haskel was named assistant principal of Ramaz, and two years later, when his father needed to step back, R. Haskel was moved up to acting principal. He began his tenure at the helm of Ramaz with a bedrock commitment to sustain his father's long-standing themes and traditions. Ramaz would continue to stand out as an open institution that warmly welcomed students from a variety of backgrounds and levels of religious observance. In the school's early years this philosophy reflected not only a matter of principle but also a recognition of the reality that few Orthodox Jews lived in the immediate vicinity of the school. In later years, as the Orthodox community of the Upper East Side grew, the percentage of students from Orthodox households increased.

R. Haskel also took care to maintain his father's emphasis on giving girls and boys the same opportunities, teaching *ivrit b'ivrit* [Hebrew language, taught in Hebrew], stressing the importance of Israel, and adhering to a consciously centrist version of Orthodoxy. At the same time, R. Haskel initiated a number of changes designed to bring Ramaz up to date with the latest educational methods. By the time he became principal, in 1971, he could announce that the school had made a successful transition "from a didactic approach to a participatory one." The teachers at Ramaz "have become listeners rather than lecturers," he wrote in a report to the parents. "Students are encouraged to be enthusiastic and active producers of education rather than mere passive products of a 'joyless classroom situation,' to quote Charles Silberman's newly coined phrase. More and more, our school is becoming student dominated and yes, even student run."

For the younger children this philosophy meant stressing "the students' needs rather than the school's curriculum" and "encouraging each child to learn at his own pace.... The teachers serve as guides and counselors." In the Upper School, juniors and seniors in a special program "study Bible and Prophets virtually on their own, with but limited guidance from teachers.... They take far fewer tests, but we are convinced that they are learning much more." In the area of secular studies too the high school underwent notable changes. "[W]e have revamped our English courses so that the students read about problems in life, in society, and in their own personal development," he reported. "The books which revolve around those problems [have thus] become much more relevant to them."

Since "it is well known that students learn more from informal educational opportunities than they do in a classroom," as R. Haskel put it, a major effort was undertaken in the spring of 1970 to increase student interest and participation in non-classroom areas as well—and "the results have been electrifying." An intensified effort to attract high school students to the voluntary morning minyan brought participation up to "about twenty five per cent of the male population of our high school" despite the fact that the minyan "begins at 7:30 in the morning—quite an 'ungodly' hour for divine worship." Attendance continued to rise during the autumn of 1970, and by the time the minyan's faculty advisor, Rabbi Mayer Moskowitz, returned several months later from an illness, "fully one-half of the student body of the high school—one hundred and fifteen boys and girls—attended the morning service. It was one of the most glorious days in the history of Ramaz, and it was organized by students alone."

Another facet of Rabbi Lookstein's "Education for Life" effort was the Senior Project, in which twelfth graders worked for two months "in some kind of educationally productive capacity" in a local hospital, public school, or other institution. A small number of seniors did take advantage of the situation in order to enjoy "a sort of senior 'cop out,'" Rabbi Lookstein conceded, but "the vast majority of the students benefited greatly from the work and brought back testimonials from the various institutions which made them and the school justifiably proud."

R. Haskel made clear in his report that political activism was an integral part of the learning process. When students want to demonstrate for Soviet Jewry or Israel, "far from trying to stifle that demand in the interests of classroom education, our policy has been that under the right auspices, students can learn more about what education really means while walking in a protest march for an hour than they can in a week of study in class." During the turmoil of the spring 1970 Kent State shootings and the escalation of fighting in Southeast Asia, Ramaz students held teach-ins and then went into the streets of the neighborhood, "trying to convince passersby of the justice of their viewpoints." "During the two weeks when these matters were at a boiling point in the country, we saw certain Ramaz students mature almost overnight," Rabbi Lookstein reported. "They became alert to the political currents of the day, sensitive to the issues, and realistic about the options open to the country and to themselves."

While R. Haskel emphasized the positive aspects of student interest in public policy, he still had to contend with the reality that segments of the KJ-Ramaz community were less than enthusiastic about the positions some of their young people were taking on the controversies of the day. For example, when college student Gilbert Kahn proposed at the 1970 annual KJ meeting that the synagogue send two telegrams to President Nixon, one supporting U.S. weapons for Israel and the other urging American withdrawal from Vietnam, the board agreed to the former but, after "a heated discussion," shelved the latter. A hint of the strong sentiments evoked by Kahn's Vietnam proposal may be deduced from the fact that R. Joseph felt compelled to appeal for "patience and calmness" and to remind the attendees "that people of all ages have opinions to express and that these opinions should be listened to with tolerance, even if we do not share such opinions."[3]

While cognizant that encouraging activism might sometimes lead to such moments of controversy within the synagogue or school, R. Haskel continued to emphasize the importance of the students' taking interest in a wide range of political and social issues. Although the plight of Soviet Jewry stood out as a topic of central concern and student activity at Ramaz throughout the 1970s and 1980s, it was by no means the only issue on their agenda. In 1979, for example, students in the Middle and Upper Schools responded to the genocide in Cambodia by holding a day of protests, prayers, and partial fasting, contributing to Cambodian refugee relief the amount they would have spent on lunch that day.[4]

It is not surprising that R. Joseph initially felt uneasy about his son's strong embrace of political activism as an educational tool. In the world to which he was accustomed, not many Orthodox Jews took part in street protests. Moreover, the antiwar movement and college campus rebellions reflected a concerted rejection of authority and tradition, and the embrace of radical social views that were alien to Orthodox Judaism. Yet he gradually came to recognize that the Jewish version of 1970s protests differed in positive ways. "My son holds that when young students march in protest, in defense of the 'prisoners of Zion' or in behalf of Anatoly Sharansky, they are actually studying Bible and performing a mitzvah greater even than the mitzvah of study," R. Joseph remarked in 1978. "He contends that marching enthusiastically and proudly in an Israel Independence Day Parade is a lesson in history, in freedom, in justice, and in Jewish solidarity. Who can differ with that? All credit to him for this practical philosophy of education."[5] In more recent years R. Haskel's philosophy has been reflected in student activities ranging from prayer services outside the Iranian Mission to the United Nations to volunteer work in New Orleans following Hurricane Katrina.

It was perhaps a reflection of Rabbi Joseph Lookstein's *menschlichkeit* toward attire, both in the classroom and in the pews of Kehilath Jeshurun, that the school dress code was one aspect of Ramaz life that R. Haskel was not willing to alter to conform to the spirit of the times. "For some time, our rules about jackets for the boys have been seriously challenged by the students," Rabbi Lookstein acknowledged in 1974. "[W]e nevertheless feel ... that a mood of dignity and reverence should prevail within [our] halls.... We are anxious to inculcate in our students a sense of 'menschlechkeit,' a quality that is often most noticeable in the younger generation by its absence." R. Haskel drew the line—but not for long. In the years to follow, not only did jackets and ties vanish, but the clothes worn by many high school students became so informal that by the spring of 1978 Principal Lookstein informed the students of a new dress code, to be implemented immediately even though it was midsemester: for the boys, no jeans, sneakers, caps, or "rugby shirts"; for the girls, no leotards, nothing sleeveless, no low-cut or tight-fitting t-shirts, and no sneakers.[6]

If attire was seen as indicative of *menschlichkeit,* an acute moral sense was even more so. Thus while his father's slogan, from Pirkei Avot, had been *Yaffeh Talmud Torah im derech eretz* [The study of Torah is beautiful when combined with *menschlichkeit*], R. Haskel's own preferred guiding slogan for the school was the midrashic statement, *Derech eretz kadma l'Torah,* which he translated as "*Menshlichkeit* precedes Torah" or, as he explained it, "Before you can be a *tzaddik,* you have to be a *mensch.*"

Nothing gave the principal more satisfaction than instances of Ramaz students exhibiting morally upstanding behavior. In a 1979 "Principal's Letter" to the parents, R. Haskel proudly reported two instances in which students found large sums of money—$500 in bills in one case, a wallet with $135 in another—and returned them to their owners while refusing to accept a reward. He took equal pleasure in a letter from a parent in 1983 recounting how when his daughter was struck by a car on the way to the school bus, another student left the bus, hailed a taxi, accompanied her to the hospital emergency room, and waited there until the child's family arrived. The parent added that it was not the first time he had heard of Ramaz students acquitting themselves so admirably, noting that recently he had heard of several students who "stopped to help an old woman who was injured or in pain on the street." The parent thanked Rabbi Lookstein for insisting that Ramaz emphasize "ethics and human responsibility."[7]

Ramaz represented only one part of R. Haskel's teaching load. From the early 1960s until 1977 he taught periodically at the Yeshiva University-affiliated Teachers Institute for Women. Beginning in the early 1970s, he occasionally substituted for his father in teaching homiletics to sophomore rabbinical students at Y.U. After his father's passing in 1979 R. Haskel taught homiletics regularly, donating his salary to the university in honor of his father's memory. Several years later, he was named Joseph H. Lookstein Professor of Homiletics. The course covered the full range of a congregational rabbi's speaking duties, such as Sabbath sermons, eulogies, wedding talks, bar and bat mitzvah remarks, and invocations. On many occasions over the years he experienced the gratification of watching a former student deliver a talk according to Looksteinian formulae, including writing out the entire speech and structuring it around three specific points of commentary.

Part of the task R. Haskel set for himself in teaching homiletics was to demonstrate to his students that the Sabbath sermon is a way of teaching the congregation, especially since many in the audience will not learn Torah anywhere else in the week to come. This perspective assumed added importance as the percentage of Orthodox congregants keenly interested in hearing the weekly sermon diminished steadily over the years. One of the first questions Rabbi Lookstein asked his students at the start of each semester was how many of them enjoy listening to sermons. Today only about one-fourth answer in the affirmative, a substantial decline from the 1960s and 1970s. "In those days people came to shul for the sermon and the davening, in that order," according to R. Haskel. "Today the sermon is peripheral." In his view, this trend represents not an ideological shift but a lifestyle change: the triumph of impatience. Just as doubleheader baseball games and double movie features are largely a thing of the past, it does not surprise him that *hashkama* minyanim—speedily recited early morning prayer services with no sermon—have become popular in many Orthodox synagogues over the years.

In addition to its educational value, the sermon serves two other important purposes, according to the Lookstein worldview. One is intellectual: it keeps the rabbi on his toes by challenging him to think deeply about a concept or issue each week. The second is practical: delivering the sermon engenders public respect for the rabbi. It validates him as an informed, thoughtful figure to whom congregants can turn during the week when issues arise or counsel is needed.

Both in his classes at Ramaz and in his sermons at KJ, Rabbi Lookstein felt no compunction about confronting hot-button issues. In 1985, for example, he began teaching a class at Ramaz in sexual ethics, precisely because it was "a subject nobody talks about." Sooner or later, he explained, Jewish teens are going to be exposed to sexual issues through the mass media or other sources, and "they have to know what is the standard of sexual behavior in American society along with the moral and halakhic issues, as well as the dangers and risks that attend that standard." The Ramaz course, jokingly referred to by the students as "Sex with the Rabbi," covered such subjects as nidda and mikveh, birth control, premarital sex, homosexuality, abortion, and AIDS. While expressing heartfelt compassion for AIDS victims, R. Haskel remained firm in rejecting the kinds of behavior that can lead to the disease. In one 1991 sermon, for example, he urged congregants to pray for the well-being of the AIDS-afflicted basketball star Magic Johnson. Yet in the same breath, the rabbi praised sports columnist Dave Anderson for being one of the few voices in the athletic world to say openly that Johnson's promiscuity "was, quite simply, immoral." R. Haskel denounced the popular perspective that all consensual sexual relations between adults are morally acceptable. "We do not subscribe to morality by majority," he said. "If the majority cheats a little on income taxes, that doesn't lessen the immorality—only the stigma." If the majority of people engage in, or approve of, promiscuity, that does not lessen its immorality. "Thank God for Dave Anderson," he concluded.[8]

Issues pertaining to gays proved to be particularly complex. R. Haskel never wavered from the Orthodox principle of rejecting homosexual practices. He publicly denounced a lesbian wedding ceremony performed by a leading Reform rabbi in 1995 as "an assault on Jewish marriage and family."[9] In a private letter to the officiating rabbi, R. Haskel made it clear he was not denouncing the women for their private behavior, but rather urging the rabbi to refrain from "celebrating something which if it were done by everybody would mark the end not alone of the Jewish people but of the human race." It was one thing to be tolerant, Rabbi Lookstein wrote, but "quite another to celebrate the lifestyle."[10] Similarly in a 1997 sermon he specifically rejected the possibility that someone could be "fully Jewish and fully gay," that one could "adopt a lifestyle that runs totally counter to Torah and insist that it be called 'fully Jewish.'"[11]

Yet in the years that followed, as he grappled with the phenomenon of gays in the Orthodox community, R. Haskel found himself looking for a more compassionate approach to the issue. He was particularly moved by the 2001 documentary *Trembling Before God*, about Orthodox gays, calling it "a magnificent film which should touch every Jew in many ways." While rejecting the film's suggestion that biblical verses prohibiting homosexuality should be reinterpreted, Rabbi Lookstein urged his congregants to "understand the pain" of Orthodox gays, "empathize" with the inner conflicts that torment them, and "love all Jews and welcome them into as full a Jewish life as they—and we—can achieve." What this meant in practical terms was that while homosexual behavior could never be acceptable, the principle of chesed requires treating a gay Jew the same as any other Jew.[12]

As the issue of gay marriage became an increasingly prominent topic of public debate, Rabbi Lookstein revisited the topic in a 2004 sermon. On the one hand, he reaffirmed his belief that gay marriage was prohibited by Judaism and harmful to society in general, and he argued that the government should not sanction such unions. At the same time, searching as always for a compassionate approach, he suggested that state and local governments could "give all kinds of people who live together in caring relationships certain privileges that would encourage those kinds of relationships ... incentives which might have a beneficial effect upon society." It was a quintessentially Looksteinian solution, one that stayed within the bounds of Jewish law while making every effort to address the real human needs at stake.[13]

## NOTES

[1] Rabbi Joseph H. Lookstein, "Rabbi Haskel Lookstein—An Evaluation and a Tribute," undated [1978], File: Rabbi Joseph Lookstein, p. 3.

[2] Rabbi Joseph H. Lookstein, "Rabbi Haskel Lookstein," op.cit., pp. 3–4.

[3] Minutes of Ninety-Eighth Annual Membership Meeting, Congregation Kehilath Jeshurun, Tuesday, May 12, 1970," pp. 7–8.

[4] "Ramaz Students Fast for Cambodians and Collect Funds for Their Relief," KJB XLVII:4 [14 December 1979], p. 1.

[5] Rabbi Joseph Lookstein, "Rabbi Haskel Lookstein," op.cit., pp. 6–7.

[6] Rabbi Haskel Lookstein, "Where We Are Now and Where We Are Headed: A Look at Ramaz at Age Thirty-Four," undated [1971], File: Ramaz, KJ.

[7] RHL, "Principal's Letter," 7 September 1979, File: Ramaz, KJ, p. 4; Rabbi Irving Greenberg to Rabbi Haskel Lookstein, 14 January 1983, File: Ramaz, KJ.

[8] Rabbi Haskel Lookstein, "AIDS Education Clarification" [letter], *Jewish Floridian*, 29 January 1988; "Ramaz Students Learn About Sex, Orthodox-Style," *Forward*, 3 April 1998; Rabbi Haskel Lookstein, "Thank God for Dave Anderson" [sermon], 16 November 1991, File: Sermons, KJ.

[9] Rabbi Haskel Lookstein, "Lesbian Marriage in Great Neck and Concubines in Brooklyn—Has the Jewish Community Gone Mad?" [sermon], 9 September 1995, File: Sermons, KJ.

[10] Rabbi Haskel Lookstein to Rabbi Jerome K. Davidson, 1 August 1995, File: Pluralism, KJ

[11] Quoted in Rabbi Haskel Lookstein, " 'Trembling Before God': The Struggle to Be Gay and Orthodox" [sermon], 10 November 2001, File: Sermons, KJ.

[12] Ibid.

[13] Rabbi Haskel Lookstein, "What Should Our Attitude Be Toward Same-Sex Marriage?" [sermon], 1 May 2004, File: Sermons, KJ.

# CONCLUSION

Making sense of senseless tragedies is one of the most difficult tasks any rabbi faces. In such situations, a congregation naturally turns to its spiritual leader for answers, but as every clergyman knows, some questions ultimately have no answers and some occurrences cannot be explained. For Rabbi Lookstein each such crisis presented anew the unique challenge of finding meaningful and effective ways to help the Ramaz-KJ family cope with the crisis. Such uniquely trying situations brought into sharp relief the qualities that characterized his career as a rabbinical and communal leader, in particular his emphasis on practical deeds of chesed to heal his community's wounds.

On the local level, the single most jarring moment occurred in 1988 when 21-year-old KJ member Alan Brown was severely injured in a swimming accident and became a paraplegic. The tragedy was compounded by the fact that Alan had just finished raising $75,000 for paralysis research in response to an auto accident that had left his best friend paralyzed. Why do such things occur? "There are no answers," R. Haskel said, "certainly not in an individual case, and one who offers them is foolish, blasphemous, and perhaps cruel." Yet, "while there are no answers, there must be a response." That response must begin with prayer, precisely at the moment when it is most difficult to pray. Second, empathy for the victim and his family, "no intrusions or pressure or overdoing it," but finding out their actual needs and meeting them. "We do not wallow in questions that have no answers. We respond with prayer, with help, and with confidence that somehow, in some way, God will help."[1]

When tragedy struck in a different community, R. Haskel's response was not very different. He and Audrey cut short their summer vacation in Florida in 2005 after a tropical storm left the region without electricity for two days. Escaping the discomforts of the blackout and settling back into their cozy Manhattan apartment and familiar daily routine, Rabbi Lookstein found himself pondering the human tendency to take life for granted and not really appreciate what one has until it is taken away. Within days that tropical storm had grown into Hurricane Katrina and destroyed much of New Orleans. "The small lessons we took from our own discomfort and dislocation were still valid," he told the congregation. "But now something much more powerful overwhelmed us." There was no way to explain why it happened, and it was certainly inappropriate for political opponents of the Bush administration to be "playing the blame game, with almost sadistic joy." The answer to the crisis was, simply, to help. "We cannot enjoy life here in New York without sharing our possessions with Jews and non-Jews who need help so desperately.... The first question I must ask is not 'What is Bush doing?' or 'What are the state and city officials doing,' but rather: What am I doing?" To that end, he announced that he and Audrey were personally contributing $1,000 to the United Jewish Communities' Katrina relief fund, and cards for pledges to the fund were distributed throughout the synagogue. "Afterwards we will pray to God for redemption and consolation," he said. "But first, we must give."[2]

A tragedy that was both national and local required a response that was national and local as well. The September 11, 2001, terrorist attacks constituted both a catastrophe on a massive scale and one that took place not in faraway Louisiana but just a few miles down the road from KJ. On the national level, Rabbi Lookstein urged his congregants to fully support the U.S. war on terrorism and recognize it as a fight against Amalek, an implacable foe that can only be destroyed, not merely weakened or imprisoned. Cumbersome airport security checks and other inconveniences would have to be endured without complaint, since America was engaged in a war comparable to the war Israel has been forced to endure for the past six decades. A spirit of patriotism and self-sacrifice was now obligatory. On the local level, the response that he recommended had to be practical. Ramaz students under the leadership of DeeDee Benel, educational director of the student activities, made 1,000 sandwiches and sent them to the rescue teams at the World Trade Center site. The congregation also raised over $75,000 for the families of nine firefighters from the fire station down the block from KJ who lost their lives in the rescue operation. The station commander and his associate were greeted at Shabbat services on Saturday morning, September 15. It was one of the most emotional moments in the history of the congregation.

There was room too for another kind of response to 9/11. The attacks were, as R. Haskel put it, "a monstrous assault on *bein adam l'chevro*," the laws governing human interaction. "It is hard to imagine a more heinous violation of elementary principles of behavior toward one's fellow man." The response, therefore, should be "to repair in some significant way our behavior" toward others, such as repairing a broken friendship, providing financial assistance to a person in need, paying bills on time, visiting the sick, and in general "just trying to be nice to everyone."[3]

If there is a single common thread in the multitude of activities and achievements that have defined Haskel Lookstein's personal life and professional career across more than seven decades, perhaps it is embodied by the response he crafted to 9/11: the application of the principle of chesed, from the arena of small interpersonal gestures to the grand stage of national and international events.

## NOTES
[1] Rabbi Haskel Lookstein, "What Shall We Do and What Shall We Say?" [sermon], 9 January 1988, File: Sermons, KJ.

2 Rabbi Haskel Lookstein, "Thoughts After a Catastrophe [After Hurricane Katrina]" [sermon], 3 September 2005, File: Sermons, KJ.

3 Rabbi Haskel Lookstein, "Our World Has Changed: Sermon the Shabbat following 'The Attack on America' 9/11/01," 15 September 2001, File: Sermons, KJ; Rabbi Haskel Lookstein, "Our World Has Changed: Remembering 9/11" [sermon], 11 September 2004, File: Sermons, KJ. The idea was communicated to the rabbi by Daniel Edelstein, a Ramaz alumnus.

# JUBILEE VOLUME PATRONS

The publication of this historic work was made possible through the generous support of the following:

Anita & Jordan Abowitz
Diane & Robert Abrams
Nicole & Raanan Agus
Lenore & Eugene Alpert
Lillian & Alan Applebaum
Barbara & Harvey Arfa
Jonathan Art
Louise & Sidney Banon
Shira & Larry Baruch and Family
Ellen Baumgarten
The Baumgarten Family
Ilana & Daniel Benson
Deborah & Barry Berg
Renee & Michael Bernstein
Barry Best
Marisa & Michael Bevilacqua
Barbara & Jonathan Blinken
The Braiterman & Mandelker Families
Mark Brecker
Devora Brickman
Ruth Brod
Deborah & Richard Born
Fran & Benjamin Brown
Doina & Lawrence Bryskin

Elias Buchwald
Tova & Norman Bulow
Roberta Caplan
Mindy & Jay Cinnamon and Family
Sherry & Neil Cohen
Carole & Seymour Cohen
Hollace & Steven Cohen
Rachel & Barry Cooper
Michelle & Eric Creizman
Vivian & Larry Creizman
Sharon Dane
Ann Davenport and Family
Rochelle & Mayer Davis
Rita & Fred Distenfeld
Elisabeth & Alan Doft
Arlene & Avrom Doft
Abigail & David Doft
Suzanne & Jacob Doft
Shlomit & Chaim Edelstein
Suzanne & Samuel Eisenstat
Randi & Howard Eisenstein and
    Family
Lillian & Elliot Eisman
Pamela & Adam Emmerich

Barbara & Abe Esses
Rebecca & Evan Farber
Estanne & Martin Fawer
Marilyn & Leonard Feingold
Miriam & Eric Feldstein
Florence & Philip Felig
Maria Finkle
Lynne & Joshua Fishman
Martine & Leo Fox
Sheila Freilich & Alan Manevitz
Anne & Natalio Fridman
Marylene & Alan Friedman
Arthur Friedman
Helen & Sidney Friedman
Ronalee & Russell Galbut
Lauren & Martin Geller
Jane & Ishaia Gol
Dale & Saul Goldberg
Tamar & Eric Goldstein
Yonina & Eric Gomberg
Ruth & David Gottesman
Trudy & Robert Gottesman
Rebecca & Laurence Grafstein
Wendy & Sholem Greenbaum
Jeanette & Mikhail Grinberg
Georgette & Steven Gross
Nicole & David Gruenstein
Rae & Stanley Gurewitsch
Jill & James Haber
Pearl & Zev Hack
Lori & Alan Harris
Hashkama Minyan of Cong. Kehilath
    Jeshurun
Fanya Gottesfeld Heller
Hedwig & Joseph Heller
Michele & Ari Hering
Kathy & Jonathan Herman
Ronnie & Samuel Heyman
Rochelle & David Hirsch
Alexandra & Moshe Hocherman
Ann & Jerome Hornblass
Mildred Hostyk
Dina & Marshall Huebner
Suzanne & Norman Javitt

Barbara & Manfred Joseph
Deborah & David Kahn
Judith & Hirshel Kahn
Ellen & Rob Kapito
Karin & Joel Katz
Keren Keshet
Barbara Braffman & Benjamin Klapper
Rosalie & Harry Kleinhaus
Ruth & Lawrence Kobrin and Family
Gloria & Richard Kobrin
Yvonne Koppel
Bertha & Henry Kressel
Randy & Mitchell Krevat
Melanie & Andrew Kule
Wilma & Stephen Kule
Vivianne & Robert Kurzweil
Seryl & Charles Kushner
Naomi Lazarus
Jane & Don Lebell
Madeleine & Mark Lebwohl
Elena, Jay, Talia, Danielle & Jacob
    Lefkowitz
Sheila & Wallace Lehman
Jane & Reuben Leibowitz
Sheila & Jeffrey Levine
Sharon & Asher Levitsky
Jane & Michael Lewittes
Jean & Armand Lindenbaum
Belda & Marcel Lindenbaum
Leora & Richard Linhart
Janice & Saul Linzer
Deborah & Robert Lipner
Judy & David Lobel
Audrey Lookstein
Joshua Lookstein
Susanna & Steven Lorch
Hannah & Edward Low
Ruth & Edward Lukashok
Jay Lunzer
Vivian & David Mark
Caroline & Morris Massel
Monica & Aaron Meislin and Family
Paula and David Menche
Perla & Julio Messer

## RAV CHESED

Mindy & Fred Miller
Naomi Miller & Bathia Churgin
Joyce & Edward Misrahi
Wendy & Adam Modlin
Frank Morgenstern
Marilyn Meltzer & Sheldon Muhlbauer
Jessica & Jason Muss
Helen & Jack Nash
Sara & Joseph Nathanson
Carol & Mel Newman
Judith & Daniel Ottensoser
Anita & Robert Payne and Family
Janelle & Sheldon Pike
Helen & Daniel Potaznik
Suzy & Larry Present
Lauren & Mitchell Presser
Dina & Douglas Propp
The Propp Family
Gabrielle Propp
Monique & Andrew Rechtschaffen
Hilda Riback
Diana & Ira Riklis
Sue & Win Robins
Pamela & George Rohr
Laurel & Lawrence Rosenbluth
Marian & William Rosner
Jennifer, Jeffry & Sam Roth
Florence & Robert Rothman
Amy & Howard Rubenstein
Naomi Ickovitz & Steven Rudolph
Victoria & Daryosh Sakhai
Susan & Martin Sanders
Evelyn & Salomon Sassoon
Sheira & Steven Schacter
Stacy & Ronald Scheinberg
Sidney Scheinberg
Paul Schulder
Janie & Robert Schwalbe
Leana & Bernard Schwartz

Erica & Robert Schwartz
Debbie & Shelly Senders and Family
Rina & Amnon Shalhov
Ruth & Irwin Shapiro
Susan & Scott Shay
Sara & Simon Shemia
Judith & Isaac Sherman
Deena & Adam Shiff
The Shudofsky Family
Alejandra & Ariel Sigal
Donna & Arthur Silverman and Family
Adina & Michael Singer
Alice Smokler
Phyllis & Mark Speiser
Melvin Stein
Robyn & David Stonehill
Surie & Robert Sugarman
Randi & David Sultan
Dorothy, Andrew, Zoe, JoBeth &
    Tanner Tananbaum
Laurie Tansman
Judith Tanz
Carla & Steven Tanz
Nadia & Yuli Tartakovsky
Susan & Robert Taub
Adele & Ronald Tauber
Elizabeth & Joshua Trump
Phyllis & Jonathan Wagner
Deborah & Raymond Ward
Diane Wassner
Grace & David Weil
Lynn Weinstein
Kim Gantz Wexler & Sanford Wexler
Judy & Philip Wilner
Rita & David Woldenberg
Barbara Zimet
Gail Suchman & Jerald Zimmerman
Cathy Zises
Seymour Zises & Andrea Tessler

Any errors and omissions will be corrected in the forthcoming complete Jubilee Volume.